*to Joan from Ian
and for Lorca and Asia
from their father*

BALI — THE ULTIMATE ISLAND

Library of Congress Cataloging-in-Publication Data

Lueras, Leonard.
Bali: the ultimate island.

1. Bali Island (Indonesia) — Description and
travel — Views.   I. Lloyd, R. Ian.   II. Title.
DS647.B2L78   1987   959.8′6   87-4968
ISBN 0-312-00863-5

Cover: A Balinese princess and a supporting cast of frog retainers pose against a studio backdrop in the south-central Bali village of Batuan. All are members of a *genggong* music and dance troupe renowned throughout the island of Bali.

Endpapers: A fanned collection of intricately illustrated *lontar* (palm-leaf books) from the Gedung Kirtya Historical Library at Singaraja, north Bali. Such books — written in Sanskrit on either dried palm leaves or on thin copper plates — recount religious, political and other historical matters dating from early times.

Frontispiece: Detail from a 1930s photograph taken during an animated *kecak* dance performance held at the village of Bona. The photographer is unknown.

Opposite title page: A *Kamasan*-style detail painting of Bali's Supreme God, Ida Sanghyang Widi Wasa. This classical icon rendering appears in a mural panel photographed inside the *Kerta Gosa,* or Hall of Justice, in the town of Klungkung.

Type was set in Benguiat by Superskill, Singapore
Color separation by Columbia and Daiichi, Singapore
Printed by Tien Wah Press, Singapore

First published in Singapore by Times Editions Pte. Ltd.
First U.S. Edition

BALI

THE ULTIMATE ISLAND

CONTENTS

DREAMING
Of Beasts, Beauties and an Island

LESS THAN TWENTY-FOUR HOURS HAD FLICKERED across the face of his silent digital watch, but during that time The Wanderer had traveled some 12,000 air miles, crossed two oceans and six time zones, dipped briefly to just about eight degrees below the equator, and, finally, in a halting rush of jumbo jet power, made it safely from one island "paradise" to another. The night before, as he prepared to board a silver and blue aircraft at Honolulu International Airport, his lady bid

him *aloha*, and gave him one last fond embrace. "Be well," she said. "And promise me that when you write your book about Bali you won't forget to describe all those special colors, sounds, smells and textures." He promised to remember such things, smiled, and walked away through one of those fluorescent-lit boarding tunnels that lead to faraway places.

Fourteen hours, four magazines, an unfinished novel and two meals later he was in Singapore. An hour-and-a-half to Jakarta, another hour-and-a-half to Denpasar, then a furious 20-minute ride in an old Chevrolet from Ngurah Rai Airport, and at long last he was in his favorite little coconut grove *losmen* at Sanur Beach. The Wanderer staggered, dazed, out of the taxi. He felt as if he had just passed through a time warp, but the sight of old friends at the inn exhilarated him. He joined the *losmen* gang for a few polite puffs on a *kretek* clove cigarette and a cold Bintang *bir*, but jet lag soon took over, and less than an hour later he fell into a humid heap on a hard mattress beneath a whirling ceiling fan. Five years had melted away since he was last inside one of these little thatched-roof bungalows, but he had once again made it back, to Bali.

In this woozy state, The Wanderer fell into a deep sleep and a series of hot, fitful dreams. He dreamed about a fight between a mean, red-spotted gecko and a small green snake. About fireflies dancing under a full moon. And about an island, somewhere east of Java, where twilight doesn't exist, where nymphs in gold foil headdresses dance spontaneously in desolate jungle clearings, and where strange, bug-eyed beasts shimmy and shake the night away. As he dreamed, a coil of mosquito punk burned slowly in a corner of his room, sending little gray streams of chrysanthemum

smoke into the thick and sultry air.

After what seemed like an eternity, but which was only a couple of hours, a dog began barking outside his door. Voices called out, "Tuan, Tuan!" and there was a knocking at his door. The Wanderer woke up bleary-eyed, wrapped a sarong around his waist, and opened the door. Outside, haloed by the orange glow of a kerosene lamp, were Wayan and Nyoman, two old surfing buddies. "*Selamat datang, B'li,*" they smiled. "Welcome back." They had heard from the *losmen* staff that he had returned to Bali. "Very important ceremony tonight. You must come with us," they said, pointing to a full moon.

The Wanderer was still half asleep, but how could he refuse such impromptu hospitality after having been away for so many years? Polite chit-chat was exchanged, *kopi bali* was ordered, and Wayan and Nyoman waited outside while he went to the *mandi* and poured cold water over his heat-soaked body.

Refreshed and re-dressed, The Wanderer joined his two friends for coffee and exchanged animated stories about Bali surfing days past. Later, as the three of them climbed onto big Binter motorcycles and roared into the night, he glanced at his watch and realized that it had been just about 23 hours since he had boarded that aircraft at Honolulu. He was only a day away from Hawaii, but the never-ending movie which is life on the island of Bali was already reeling by.

About 10 kilometers of dark roads later, he found himself in a large community temple in a small countryside village whose name he cannot now recall. Some kind of misfortune had visited this village in recent months, so tonight, on a full moon date deemed propitious for the exorcising of evil spirits, this particular village was pulling out all its spiritual stops.

Balinese dream sequences come in all sorts of shapes, hues and colors. One moment you'll encounter a lone shepherd and an orderly platoon of ducks flashing by at sunset time (preceding pages), then when night falls the dream may take the form of a dancing, prancing Jauk (left). Beauty often meets beast on the startling island of Bali.

In the temple's outer courtyard, a lion-like *barong* was chattering at a fanged *Rangda* witch with pendulous black and white breasts, while in another area, little children made up like painted dolls laughed and giggled at the satirical antics of a *dalang* shadow puppet master. Soaring above these two theater forms were the ringing bronze sounds of a full ensemble *gamelan* playing fine percussive music at full orchestral tilt. Balinese of all ages milled about the temple in their most elegant brocade and batik *kains*, and fragrances of incense, frangipani and jasmine perfumed the night air. It was almost too much to take on one's first evening back in Bali.

Several hours later, The Wanderer was back in his room, wondering why he had ever left this place. "Yes, dear," he thought to himself. "I won't forget to write about all those special colors, sounds, smells and textures." As the pink light of another Bali dawn began glowing in the east, he counted the calls of a dozen crowing roosters and once again fell asleep.

The Wanderer truly enjoyed his dreaming in Bali. He savored those fantasy-filled lapses in sleep that quietly marked the end of yet another day spent puttering around under the hot, equatorial sun. Night after night, after slow, unplanned days spent doing nothing in particular, he would work, play and dine away the hours between sunset and midnight. Then when the air was cool and invigorating, he would set out on long and meditative walks along the beach, back roads and main street of Sanur. Once he was thoroughly exhausted, he would return home, cool himself with a bath, and curl up in bed with a good book.

Before blowing out his reading lamp, he would ritually pop a cassette tape of Balinese music into a small battery-powered sound system that was automatically timed to switch off an hour later. As this recorded *gamelan* music crashed and tinkled in the dark, he would recall in sequence all that had happened to him on the island during the day. Slowly, soothingly, he would fall into a delicious first dream, and, on automatic cue, the *gamelan* recording would soon click off. It was a neatly planned and electronically programmed finale to his daily routine on Bali, but he loved it immensely. After all, he thought, what is "Paradise" if not a perfectly edited and scored dream, a living video tape as it were, swimming with hedonistic expectations that can be stopped, reversed, speeded up, slowed down or frozen still, depending on whim.

Fortunately for some, but unfortunately for some others, that has long been the case with Bali. During the past 400 years or so since the island was "discovered" by the West, Bali has become, for better or for worse, a dream island favored by happily indolent paradise-seekers. Its name alone evokes strong, romantic feelings of exotica, beauty, mystery and unreality. And over the years, as more and more dreamers and wanderers visited the island, the more beautiful and unrealistic she has become. Indeed, since long-range jet aircrafts first began arriving at the island's international airport in the late 1960s, this dream has become increasingly more accessible.

As these travelers return to the real world, stock epithets about Bali such as "Heaven on Earth," "The Last Paradise" and "Island of the Gods" are repeated over and over in foreign cocktail circles, and before you can hum a few lingering bars of Rodgers and Hammerstein's "Bali Hai," even more people find themselves packing up and enthusiastically booking flights bound for this remote, emerald landfall where honey-skinned natives commune with wild-eyed gods in an Eden-like setting. Once such armchair dreamers have been here, they either fall madly in love with the place, vowing to return again one day, or they return home with stories about how "Paradise" has finally been ruined. As budget traveling Australians so curtly put it, they leave bored, having "been there" and "done that." Paradise Found. Paradise Erased.

Perhaps it is because of such Paradise-bashing that The Wanderer enjoyed his sleeping and dreaming so much. By dreaming, he could avoid the cynicism and bitchiness of people *who don't understand*. And in that pleasant, free-floating state of mind and body, he didn't have to think too much about the untoward realities of life in a place like Bali. Indeed, why pop this beautiful bubble by reading about the sad wars, pestilences, drugs and natural and man-made disasters that have periodically torn Bali apart during this century? Why consider the specter of back-stooping labor under the equatorial sun, the island's high incidence of domestic violence, devastating volcanic eruptions, and the local anti-Communist bloodbaths of 1965 and 1966 during which people ran amok and brutally murdered more than 100,000 of their own island neighbors? Why dwell on such negative things

*A **daily** mandi, or bath, is part of every Balinese person's routine.*
These particular women are refreshing themselves in the sacred
waters of a communal bathing pool in the highland village of Sebatu.

when with the click of a tape-recorder switch you can drown them out and instead simply revel in the scent of thousands of fruits and flowers, beautiful bronze bodies, mysterious rituals and music, fine surfing waves and the soothing balm of breezes blowing off the surrounding Indian Ocean and Java Sea?

The Australian historian-author Gavan Daws has written in a 1980 book about Polynesia entitled *Dream of Islands* (W.W. Norton & Company) that it is the *idea* of an island, not necessarily the island itself, that has long drawn white men to the South Seas and other tropical places they call "Paradise." They are attracted to such islands, Daws says, because such idylls represent the "other side" of their own psyche and world. The mere act of going to such a place becomes an exotic, vicarious "journey into the self." Such islands exert a special, mysterious pull "away from continents, from civilization, toward ease, voluptuousness, [and the] warm beauty of place and people." In effect, they represent a dream outside oneself.

While reading that book one evening, The Wanderer was reminded of the time of the French impressionist artist Paul Gauguin, when French Polynesia, and particularly the island of Tahiti, enjoyed the sort of mystique still accorded Bali. Shortly before his death in the Marquesas in 1903, Gauguin, who was terminally ill at the time, wrote a letter back to his sales agent in Paris in which he complained that he was tired of the South Seas and wanted to return to Europe. Do not come back, his agent advised. "At this moment you are that extraordinary, legendary artist who from the depths of Oceania dispatches his disconcerting, inimitable works ... ." The agent complained, probably wisely, that if Gauguin returned, his hard-earned mystique would become a discernible reality and he would be finished as a viable and eminently marketable artist. His presence in Paris would expose him as a mere mortal and kill the "dream" that people had of him as a noble, white savage in the tropics.

In many ways that is the situation in Bali today. Despite prying, censorious eyes, modernization and instant, satellite-relayed communications systems, Bali, its people and their rich culture are still far away, mysterious and alive in a legendary sort of way. Travelers from the Americas and Europe still have to invest considerable time and money to get here, so the dream — as *idea* and *island* — is still intact.

From a highway viewpoint *near Rendang, the hazy cone of Bali's sacred Gunung Agung rises*
high (3,142m) above serpentining rice terraces. In Bali's complex cosmology, Gunung
Agung or "Supreme Mountain," the island's highest mountain, is the "Navel of the Universe"
and the throne and resting place of Bali's Supreme God, Ida Sanghyang Widi Wasa.
Following pages: Dawn glows across the nearly perfect cone shape of Gunung Agung,
Bali's most sacred peak, as seen from Penelokan.

To obtain heavenly elixir, amerta, the gods sent Anantabhoga to uproot mighty Mandara mountain. The tortoise Akupa went under the milky sea, to be the fulcrum on which the mountain would rest. "Be kind, great ocean, and let your waters be parted by this island. Great will be the rejoicing in the three worlds when amerta has been distilled." Divine serpent Basuki was the rope, wound about Mandara mountain. As the rope was pulled the mountain would turn to churn the milky sea.

King of the gods Indra sat, steadying the mountain, on its peak. Ready to begin work, the gods held the tail end of the serpent, the demons its head. As they pulled in turns, poisoned fire appeared in the snake's hot breath. But their striving did not diminish, as both sides struggled mightily, joyously, to obtain the elixir. The sea rumbled as thunder, and all nature on Mandara mountain was in turmoil for the churning...

— from a Balinese version of the *Adiparwa,* the creation sequence and first book of the great *Mahabarata* epic. Translation by Mary Zurbuchen and I Wayan Wija.

One popular nickname given Bali is "The Morning of the Earth." This appellation lends itself to varying moods and colors, depending on where you are as another Balinese dawn breaks. If you are at Candidasa on the island's east coast (preceding pages), the scenery can take on a mauve hue. But if you are in the cool heights of Kintamani (above and right), the color is cool blue and clinging grey.

Once the sun burns early morning mists away, the landscape on most of the island turns a dazzling emerald green, amber or rust, depending on which local rice-growing cycle you are passing through. Following pages: A lone field hand surveys the lush, piano-shaped terraces of a hillside sawah growing somewhere east of Klungkung.

At Kubutambahan, just east of Singaraja on Bali's north coast, a lone pemangku *priest clad in white (preceding pages) walks past the split gate* (candi bentar) *of the Pura Medrwé Karang, the "Temple of the Owner of the Land." This pyramidal temple is a fine example of the vigorous style of northern Balinese architecture.*

Rangda, "the witch-widow mistress of black magic," makes a grotesque appearance wherever you turn in Bali, in this case (left and above) in a temple at Penebel. Following pages: A woman heads for the busy Denpasar market; the Denpasar market hums with early-morning activity; and white-capped religious devotees march to a temple along the main street of Ubud.

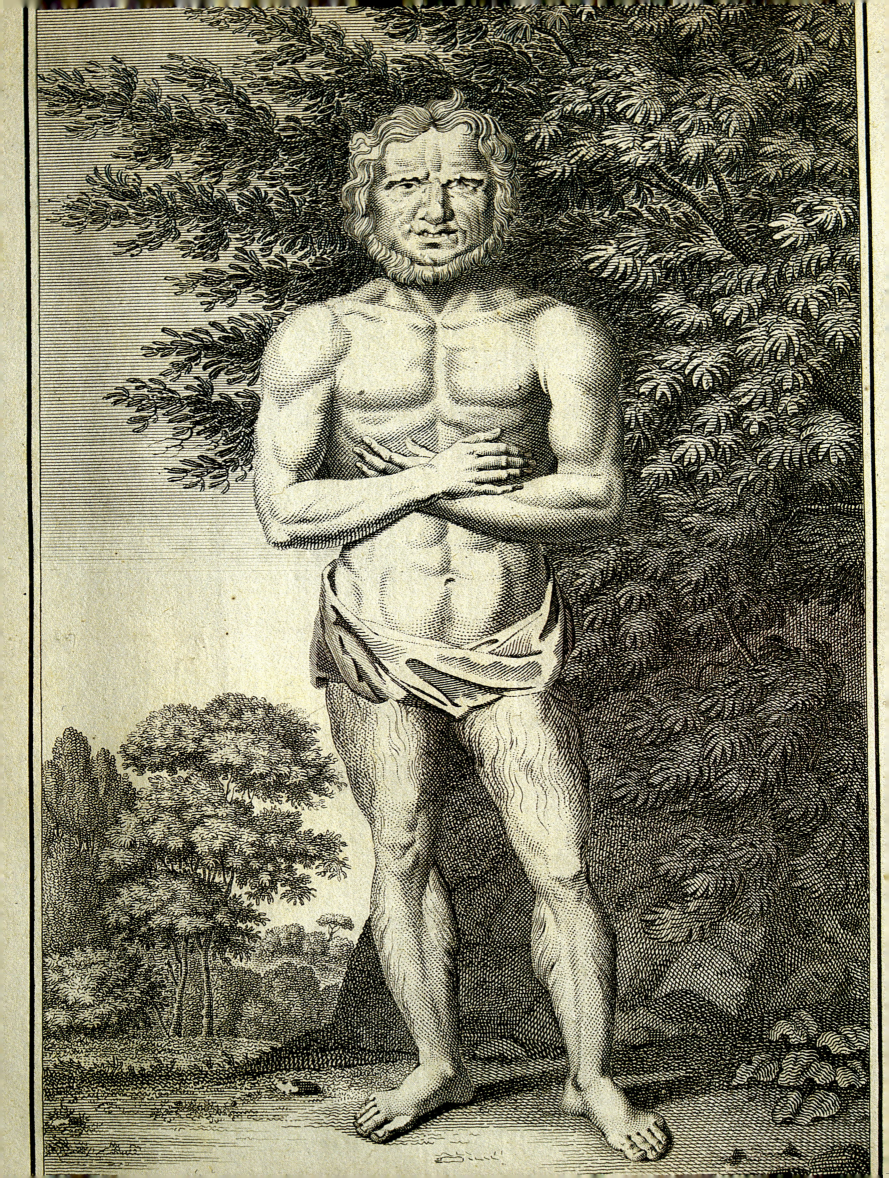

ANCIENT BALI
When Men and Gods Were One

UNDERSTANDABLY, AND IN KEEPING WITH THE complex mix of animism, ancestor worship and Hindu-Buddhist beliefs that govern daily life and religion here, the Balinese people have traditionally accorded great respect to the so-called high places that rise prominently here and there above their small island. Whether this has a pyschological link to ancient forms of volcano worship or is simply a symbolic Olympus-like deference to Heaven as a great height, one thing is emi-

nently clear: every person on this island who considers himself or herself to be Balinese is obsessed — physically and spiritually — with the idea that higher forms of life, or cosmic energy, reside in the mountains. Up There is The Power, The Omniscient Almighty, that keeps everything below in check.

Not unlike today's astronomers who direct highly sophisticated, infrared scanning devices toward galaxies, quasars or extraterrestrial life in search of new scientific truths, the Balinese also utilize special sighting devices to zero in on their particular concepts or visions of the universal cosmos. These sighting devices, in the form of ancestral shrines called *padmasana*, are found in nearly every temple or housing compound on the island, and each one is carefully aimed toward the active Balinese volcanoes of Gunung Batur and Gunung Agung. From a distance they really do look like notched rifle sights, but up close you will find that these *padmasana* or "eight-leafed lotus seats" are basalt stone constructions that have been precast or sculpted into the shapes of tiny seats or thrones. These chairs rest on sculpted turtle platforms and are usually flanked by two writhing dragons. Below, three-tiered platforms support the whole works, and, at the very top, floating in space, is a painted or sculpted image of Bali's Supreme God, Ida Sanghyang Widi Wasa, who according to Balinese mythology resides in and about the summit of Bali's highest and most holy mountain, Gunung Agung (3,142 m). Sanghyang Widi, also known as Tintia, or Sanghyang Tunggal, is usually represented in traditional iconography as a white-and-nude male figure surrounded by orange-red flames that emanate from his vital body parts and extremities. He is *the* Great One who hovers over all, keeping check on the forces

of Good and Evil, Positive and Negative, Black and White and so on in the Past, Present and as yet indiscernible (to humans) Future. His home base is Gunung Agung, the exalted "Supreme Mountain" which the Balinese proudly call the "Navel of the Universe".

Below Sanghyang Widi — within the grand, geological scheme of atoms, neutrons, protons and magical elixirs that join other elements to make up our planet Earth — is the baby of an island called Bali. Not unlike the ubiquitous toddlers you see being carried here and there about Bali, this infant island is just beginning life. And like Bali's human babies, she wears magical neck amulets that contain part of her umbilical cord. These magical amulets are the still active volcanoes that originally created — and are still creating — this equatorial island.

According to scientists who determine such things, Bali's volcanoes did not even begin to exist until sometime between 10,000 and 100,000 years ago. To the human mind that may seem like eons ago, but in purely geological terms it is but a wink in time. Conversely, Bali is, landwise, but one tiny and twinkling star in that vast galaxy of equatorial atolls and islands known as the Indonesian archipelago.

At the onset of Bali's fiery birth, tens of thousands of years before enlightened Vedic scholars in faraway India composed the poetical stanzas of the *Mahabharata-Adiparwa* creation chant, a series of great, Mandara-like mountains did indeed turn on their fulcrums and cause waters of the nearby Indian Ocean to rumble, thunder and churn in a mad, milky turmoil. During these active millennia, beginning sometime during the later Pleistocene Epoch and continuing into the Holocene (or Recent) Epoch, local waters were parted and savaged by vast quantities of white hot magma being

Many early European depictions of things Balinese were pure fantasy, based only on dated descriptions carried home by early explorers. An engraving entitled Malais de l'Isle de Baly *(left) appeared in a French book,* Histoire de Voyages, *published in 1750, and a cremation drawing (above) was reproduced in an early Dutch book.*

released by the earth's magnetic and incandescent core. These primary matters burst out of moving vents on the ocean floor, then boiled to the sea's surface in a frenzy of gigantic steam geysers, poisonous gases and awesome apocalyptic explosions that eventually cooled down and added to the string of more than 13,600 islands that stretch some 5,120 kilometers across the vast Indonesian archipelago. As the *Adiparwa* creation sequence sings, all nature in this equatorial region, along this part of the world's Asia-Pacific Rim of Fire, "was in turmoil for the churning."

In this particular place, an island that extends east-west from longitude 114° 26' to 115° 42' East, and north-south from latitude 8° 4' to 8° 52' South, emerged a series of so-called strato volcanoes, or exploding mountain peaks, that set to work — passively during cooling-off periods and actively during occasional bursts of infernal temperament — to create a ragged splotch of land that measures roughly 150 kilometers wide and 80 kilometers high. Sometime during the past thousand years this volcanic island just south of the equator became known to early residents and travelers as Po'li, Baly, Bale or, more recently, Bali.

Once Bali's fire-breathing dragons were in place on their turtle fulcrums, they begin sculpting, in concert with prevailing winds, rains and a pounding seashore, the island's many snaking waterways, arid northern deserts, fertile southern lowlands and undulating central and eastern highlands. The consequence of all this vulcanism and erosion is a subtropical landmass of 5,564 square kilometers that has assumed the shape of a prehistoric fish fossil with a hydrofoil stabilizer (the Bukit peninsula) at its midsection. This ancient petroglyph fish swims almost exactly due east in blue-green waters only 1.6 kilometers east of Java, about 24 kilometers west of the next Indonesian island of Lombok, and approximately 1,200 kilometers due northwest of the vast Australian subcontinent.

If you look at a good relief map of Bali, you will discover that this fish-shaped island's clearly visible "eye" is the kilometer-wide crater of the isle's principal volcano, Gunung Agung. Gunung Apat (314 m) on the western extremity forms the tail fin, Kubutambahan to the north is the dorsal fin, Gunung Seraya (1,175 m) and the coastal lowlands to the east are the friendly snout, while curving Padangbai on the southeast coast is the whimsical mouth. Due south of Padangbai and

the coal black sands of Kusamba are three smaller sister islands — Nusa Penida, Nusa Lembongan and Nusa Ceningan, which like Bali's southern Bukit peninsula are not volcanic in composition, but are masses of marine limestone that were pushed above sea level by volcanic activity. These offshore islets have become popular vacation hideaways and surfing resorts in recent years, although in earlier days they were deemed haunted and fit only for outcasts, including criminals, political exiles and other undesirables.

Coincidentally, or perhaps appropriately, this small but now world-renowned island called Bali sits on the cusp of one of the world's most interesting transitional evolutionary zones. It was exactly due east of Bali, in the strait that separates the island from Lombok, that Alfred Russel Wallace (1823–1913), an eminent English naturalist, drew what has become known in evolutionary science circles as Wallace's Line. This arbitrary line marks the demarcation point where the flora and fauna of subtropical Southeast Asia make a sudden and quite dramatic transition into the plants and animals typical of Australasia. Wallace, a contemporary and sometime colleague of another Englishman, Charles Darwin (1809–1882), presented his findings about these life changes in a joint paper with Darwin in 1858. Darwin was to release his landmark (and controversial) work on evolution entitled *The Origin of Species* the following year.

Following visits to this part of the world, first during the 1850s and later during the early 1860s, Wallace's findings received proper, international attention when his exhaustive book about this region — *The Malay Archipelago, The Land of the Orang-utan and the Bird of Paradise, A Narrative of Travel with Studies of Man and Nature* — was published in 1868 by Macmillan and Co., London. In that grand, geographical study, Wallace wrote the following about these two islands "which form the Austro-Malayan division" of Southeast Asia's Indo-Malay archipelago:

The great contrast between the two divisions of the Archipelago is nowhere so abruptly exhibited as on passing from the island of Bali to that of Lombock, where the two regions are in closest proximity. In Bali we have barbets, fruit-thrushes, and woodpeckers; on passing over to Lombock these are seen no more, but we have an abundance of cockatoos,

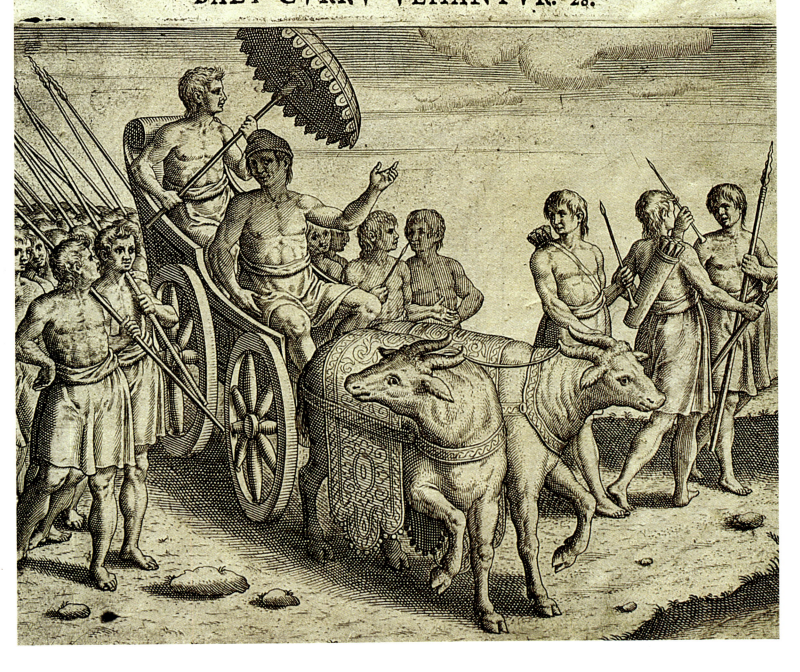

QVOMODO REGES INSVLAE
BALY CVRRV VEHANTVR. 28.

*"Here you see the **King of Bali,** who showed us much friendship, and this is the way he rides on his Royal Wagon, which is pulled by two white buffaloes. His guards carry spears with gilded points through which they also blow darts." From the first official Dutch account of the Cornelis de Houtman trading voyage to Bali in 1595.*

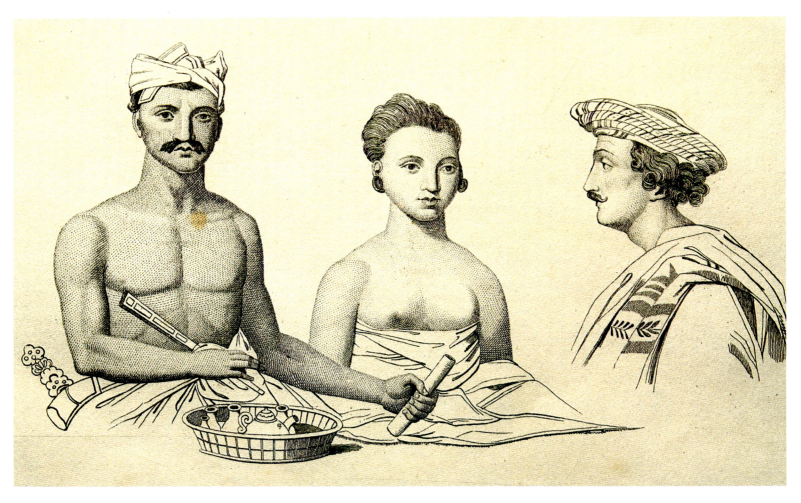

honeysuckers, and brush-turkeys, which are equally unknown in Bali, or any island further west. The strait is here fifteen miles wide, so that we may pass in two hours from one great division of the earth to another, differing as essentially in their animal life as Europe does from America. If we travel from Java or Borneo to Celebes or the Moluccas, the difference is still more striking. In the first the forests abound in monkeys of many kinds, wild cats, deer, civets, and otters, and numerous varieties of squirrels are constantly met with. In the latter none of these [animals typical of tropical Asia] occur … .

Thus, in a very real sense, Bali is the last frontier in this part of Asia for those looking for a lost, tropical paradise. From here on, and until you reach the fringing reefs of Melanesia and Polynesia, brown — not jungle green — is the predominant land color. You probably won't find a kangaroo hopping about in Lombok's bush, but according to Lombokphiles, you will spot "new" creatures such as primitive anteaters, sulphur-crested cockatoos, rozella parrots, large mountain lizards and the kind of lovebirds you would expect to see on a tree in the Australian outback.

Back in the Sixties, when the so-called "Hippie Trail" was busy with backpackers wending their way overland to Asia from Europe, Bali was, appropriately, the last place where these colorful nomads stopped for rest and recreation before beginning their journey home.

Like explorers who visited this place more than 400 years ago, these latter-day dharma bums returned with fantastic stories about a beautiful place with a vibrant living culture, attractive people, bearable living costs, pristine beaches and, in deference to modern needs, perfectly curling surfing waves.

The plants, flowers and land and sea animals of Bali are sometimes romanticized by visiting travel writers, but in fact they are not really all that different from what you might find in the wilds of nearby Java or Malaysia. Little, if anything, living on Bali is endemic. Nearly all life was imported — either by winds, sea currents or man — during the many thousands of years following the island's original vulcanism. Grand but brooding banyans with destructive adventitious roots create a tangle here and there, as do flaming coral trees and occasional stands of teak, mahogany, casuarina and pine, but probably the first plant to establish itself here was the useful coconut palm, which, as on most tropical islands, probably sprouted like a green feather duster from coconuts that floated into the island on sea currents and took root along the island's reef-fringed and inhospitable coastlines.

Chattering monkeys shriek and carry on like spoiled children in forest areas, and on nearly every wall you will find a scampering gecko. These white-and-red spotted lizards are harmless enough, but urbane tourists cringe when they hear its repetitious, Godzilla-like clucking during their first night in Bali.

A small Balinese tiger (*Panthera tigris balica*) used to pad about in Bali's forested highlands, but apparently this critter spotted his last big game hunter sometime in the late 1930s. These days the only time you will ever see one of those toothy tigers is in an old-style *wayang*-Kamasan painting for sale in an art gallery. A similar fate apparently awaits Bali's rare river crocodiles and a wild species of buffalo called *banteng*. There are still wild deer and bush pigs around, but the only real denizens that still proliferate here are snakes, of the poisonous and non-poisonous varieties. "Aduh!, Yikes!" say visitors, but then again what would Paradise be without the occasional serpent.

Of interest to birdwatchers is the island's only indigenous bird, the now extremely rare white starling (*Leucopsar rothschild*), known to locals as the *Jalak Putih*. This bird is a kind of mynah, but, according to ornithologists, it is in a genus entirely its own. It is generally lumped into the mynah-starling-quackle family of birds, and is sometimes specifically referred to as a Rothschild's quackle or Rothschild's mynah, but its favored name is, simply, the Bali starling. Seriously threatened by extinction, the white starling's population is now estimated to be at around 120 to 150, and is confined to only a very small area of the Bali Barat National Park and nature reserve in the northwest corner of Bali. Indeed, jaded birdwatchers all but weep when they spot one flitting about in Bali's bush.

Victor Mason, an active birdwatcher-cum-publican who lives in the Balinese town of Ubud, waxes almost poetic when describing the Balinese white starling. "The really stunning thing about it," he says, "is its brilliant light cobalt-blue facial skin, or mask, if you will. Absolutely beautiful! And when this bird is in flight — or preening itself — you see these wonderful black bands on the tips of all the flight feathers of the wings and the tail. Otherwise, it's almost snow-white. It's a very stunning bird." Mason reports that there is speculation that the Java sparrow may have originated in Bali, and that there could also be an original Bali babbler, but he concedes that the white starling is probably the island's "only truly endemic bird."

Bali's birds, bees and *banteng* are all very interesting, but no informed discussion of Bali's wildlife would be complete without at least a passing comment about the island's most ubiquitous indigenous creature, the much maligned Bali dog. Indeed, when it comes to animal life, one could literally say that Bali has long ago gone to the dogs. No first time visitor to Bali will ever forget his or her initial encounters with one or more of those ugly creatures with its straight tail, short hair and uniformly squat body.

These truly unattractive canines are seen everywhere on the island — generally mucking about in packs, barking and howling threateningly in the night, growling menacingly from temple or house gates, and gobbling up anything edible that hits the ground. Dogs may be "man's best friend" in other parts of the world,

A handsome trio of "Balinese Inhabitants" with decidedly European faces (left) appeared in an early 19th-century German publication, while a stylized drawing of a seven-roofed Balinese meru temple (above) was reproduced in a French travel volume released in 1832.

but here in Bali they are generally treated with derision and seen as something of a necessary evil.

According to Lian Wirawan, the wife of a Denpasar medical doctor who is known on the island as a sort of one-person Balinese humane society, Bali's unusual dogs are mongrelized descendants of an original wild dog that has been on the island since ancient times. They long ago became known to the Balinese as *cecing kacang*, or "peanut dogs," because they were traditionally kept around Balinese homes as living sewerage disposal units. Before the introduction of proper toilets in some Balinese households, these dogs' primary function in a typical living compound was — and still is — to eat various human and other organic waste matters deposited in backyard toilet sites. A secondary function, which the dogs no doubt enjoy more, is their lowly role as offerings eaters. Like swooping vacuum cleaners, these dogs roam about the village and gobble up the rice and other little morsels that the Balinese place every morning and evening on little banana- and palm-leaf trays on the roadside and in and about their homes and temples. Some Balinese say they welcome this part of a dog's life, because by allowing these lowly creatures to eat such household offerings they are regularly placating potentially inimical spirits that have returned to life in the form of a four-legged and fanged scavenger.

Wirawan says that though nearly all of these dogs look alike, "short and ugly," many of them have over the years become genetically mixed with other types of dogs that were introduced to Bali during the past few centuries. In the mountain area of Kintamani, for example, she says there are quite a number of Bali dogs that bear a slight resemblance to *chow-chow* dogs brought to Bali by early Chinese immigrants. And around Denpasar you will sometimes spot a larger, slightly more handsome mutt which she says are the accidentally cross-bred descendants of Alsatian guard dogs shipped in by Japanese military forces that occupied Bali during World War II.

Perhaps the most curious of Bali's evolved mongrels, however, can be seen in the honky-tonk resort community of Kuta. These critters are an unusual spotted variety of the Bali peanut dog and are said to be the great-great-great grandpuppies of a pack of Dalmatians that roamed Kuta during the time of the legendary Danish "White Rajah" of Bali named Mads Johan-sen Lange. Lange, a successful trader who was based in Kuta from 1839 until his death there in 1856, imported a number of purebred Dalmatians to Bali during his years on the island, and today, some 130 years after Lange's passing, those little spotted things yapping at you as you make your way down a dark *kampung* lane are a lingering reminder of his once powerful trading empire and dog kennel.

Physically, Bali isn't all that different from a host of other volcanic islands in this part of the world that were lost and later found. Like most islands to its east and west, Bali is dominated by smouldering volcanoes, rivers that zigzag through green valleys, and palm-fringed beaches that bark with the crash of every wave. Indeed, many of Indonesia's jungly, equatorial islands would provide a near-perfect setting for a Hollywood film sequel to movies such as "Raiders of the Lost Ark," "King Kong" or "South Pacific."

Perhaps the most unusual of Bali's geographical sites are the four mountain lakes — Bratan, Buyan, Tambelingan and Batur — that add a cool blue relief to the forest-rimmed saddles that sprawl between Bali's western and eastern highlands. One of these lakes, Batur, sits at the foot of Gunung Abang (2,150 m) in a prehistoric caldera that is 450 meters deep and about 11 kilometers wide. Within its usually placid confines rises the still active peak of Gunung Batur (1,717 m), which in 1917 and 1926 blew its top and killed some 1,300 people and destroyed an estimated 65,000 homes and 2,500 temples. If you are intrepid enough to climb up and look into Batur's cone, you will smell noxious sulphur fumes, spot steam vents here and there, and sense, in a quietly eerie sort of way, that this particular hot spot could at any moment begin rippling with the ominous and trembling prelude to a volcanic eruption called "harmonic tremor."

Beyond these highland waterways, where unusual mountain outrigger canoes flit hither and thither like day-glow waterbugs, the island is a typical, tropical complement of natural phenomena not quite unlike similar places in the South Seas, Caribbean or Indian Ocean. What is most impressive about Bali — and indeed what distinguishes her from every other island "paradise" in the world — is the way man has evolved here, and how he has painted, carved, ploughed and planted this place into his own vision of godliness. To use an old cliché, Bali is truly one of those

rare places on earth that had to be invented to exist.

The island's geology, botany and animal life are all easy enough to explain and comprehend, but when it comes to man, well, that's another matter entirely. As effusive Hollywood scriptwriters are fond of gushing, this place is "a universe unto itself" where "everything is touched by magic," and where people "work dreamily, rhythmically, never straining a muscle … ."

Because the island's offshore waters have long provided a formidable natural barrier to outsiders in the form of treacherous coral reefs and tricky sea currents, and also because the island has always had a dearth of suitable anchorages, foreign seafarers usually bypassed Bali for more accessible and safer havens. Consequently, the original people who settled here were generally well-protected and naturally isolated from outside encroachments. Even the imperious Dutch, who had been firmly established in nearby Java for more than three centuries, warily postponed significant military movements against the isolated Balinese until early in this century because it was simply too much of a hassle to land there.

Historians and anthropologists have long been curious as to why nearly all of the island's oldest communities — places like Sembiran, Julah, Kintamani and Trunyan — are located in harsher and colder highland areas rather than in the more temperate and accommodating lowlands. Were the original inhabitants driven to these fortress-like mountain areas by earlier invaders? Were they simply partial to a San Francisco-like climate? Or was this simply an expression of their animistic interest to remain close to ancestral gods whose spirits, according to tradition, reside in and around Bali's volcanic peaks? One theory contends that the early Balinese retreated to these places following the occurrences of a series of massive *tsunamis* (or tidal waves) that devastated lowland areas during earlier periods in their history. Such occurrences were highly likely in centuries past, following cataclysmic eruptions on neighboring Indonesian islands. It is a theory that may also explain in part why the Balinese have traditionally regarded the sea as the abode of vicious, wrathful demons, and why they have always revered the mountains, or high places, as safe and holy places. As the Mexican artist-anthropologist Miguel Covarrubias wrote some fifty years ago (in his book *Island of Bali*), the Balinese "are one of the rare island peoples in the world who turn their eyes not outward to the waters, but upward to the mountain tops."

More recently, geologists, religionists and even anthropologists have attributed the Balinese people's traditional awe of high places to the origin phenomena discussed earlier. They point out that when the tortoise Akupa stirs under the Milky Sea, and the divine serpent Basuki begins breathing fire, all nature is indeed "in turmoil for the churning." Mountains move, monkeys shriek, and man pays very special attention to what is happening up there on Mandara Mountain.

This early upside-down map of Bali (above) was published by the Dutch East India Company in 1725. It was orginally drawn by François Valentine, the Company's official recorder. Following pages: A Balinese gamelan plays music and another woman fuels the flames as the widow of a Balinese nobleman commits suttee, or ritual self-immolation. Early accounts of such "barbaric" customs infuriated the sensibilities of people back home in Holland.

n: 42

CONTACT
With Curious, Outside Worlds

TIDAK! NO! NEVER! THERE IS NO WAY THAT WE will give in to your demands and lose our sovereignty. We would rather die!" The grand Tjokorda, the Rajah of Badung (Denpasar), preened and strutted nobly as his words were sung for him by a presiding *dalang*. As the *dalang* moaned in a musical falsetto, and the Rajah mimed his part in stylized dance, a complete *gamelan gong kebyar* speeded up its thundering orchestral voice. Percussive bronze resounded throughout the spacious

auditorium, and the Rajah took the musical cue splendidly. Radiating pride and sultanic opulence, he rose on his toes, turned, bristled, and then rush-danced toward the upturned noses of a pith-helmeted Dutch Controleur and his leering and mustached *aide-de-camp* in blue great coat and gold-braided epaulets. He taunted and teased the Dutch officials, daring them to touch him. He then bristled one last time, turned his back on the two Dutchmen, and danced defiantly back to the Balinese side of the stage. In a patriotic response to the Rajah's grand flourish of anti-colonial temper, the more than 2,000 Balinese in the audience erupted into whistles and cheers. As the din died, the *gamelan* ensemble changed musical gears and segued into a bold and somber marching movement. What was a bold and bronze orchestral attack became a dirge, and with that change in musical tempo the two haughty and thoroughly insulted Dutchmen harrumphed, clicked their leather boots, and strode imperiously off the stage through a rear, splitgate (*candi bentar*) exit.

"Okay, Okay. You have it your way. But be careful, Tjokorda." The Controleur shook a finger at the Rajah and hissed in his guttural tongue — and the audience jeered, whistled and catcalled in amused response.

The next scene was introduced by a wild staccato of offstage simulated explosions. Gunshots rang out, the *gamelan* fired up again, and out marched a platoon of blue-jacketed Dutch soldiers carrying wooden rifles. In deference to Balinese-style theatrics, the *orang putih* wore large "European" *topeng* noses and march-danced to the martial airs of a *baris gede* warrior's dance. But instead of spears, they thrust toy rifles into the air to exhibit their macho prowess. The crowd again broke into jeers, then burst into laughter as the

Dutch Controleur reviewed and comically upbraided his bumbling troops.

Later in this very remarkable performance, however, the assembled Balinese turned almost eerily silent as the Rajah, his male and female courtiers and a company of spear-carrying warriors paused to wrap their bodies in white cotton mourning sashes. They were preparing — with prayers and offerings — for a last act of mass ritual suicide. The *gamelan* and *dalang* wailed ominously, dolefully, and a few moments later the *puputan*, "the end," begin. Big-nosed Dutch bluejackets sneak - attacked from stage right, stage left, backstage and even through auditorium exits.

The Balinese, meanwhile, fought valiantly, but many of them, mostly women, simply drew golden kris daggers from their white waist sashes and dramatically thrust them into their necks and abdomens. After about two minutes of screams, gunshots, chaos and fierce suicidal fighting, the stage proper was littered with elegantly costumed bodies of Balinese royalty, priests, warriors and loyal retainers. Only a few Dutch lay still in this gold-and-brocade killing field.

In the aftermath of this dramatized carnage strode in the avenged Dutch Controleur. At first he was pleased by his decisive military victory, but after surveying the extent of the destruction, he turned to his aide and asked aloud: "My God! What have we done?" With those words, the lights of north Denpasar's Dharma Graha government performing *wantilan* went dark.

When the stage lights flashed back on, and the assembled cast had taken a final curtain call bow, the gathered crowd began filing out. It was the night of September 20, 1986, and in proper style — with music, dance and traditional stage offerings — the Balinese of Badung (Denpasar) had just completed an annual

The demure legong dancer (left) was photographed in about 1922 by Thilly Weissenborn (1889–1964), the daughter of a German coffee-grower based in Kediri, east Java. Weissenborn's many fine portraits are well-documented, but the photographer who took the regal portrait of the "Rajah of Sukawati-Ubud" (above) is unknown.

Sendratari Puputan Badung performance to commemorate the 80th anniversary of the great Badung *puputan* of September 20, 1906. It was a poignant and historical reenactment by Balinese, for Balinese, and neither a tourist — nor Dutchman — was to be seen anywhere in the spacious, open-air auditorium.

It is perhaps appropriate that the Balinese choose to commemorate this gruesome event in private, because, as all Balinese know, the 1906 *puputan* really was The End. It was a historical turning point, or final act, that marked the passing of old Bali and the beginning of a modern era that has been fraught with culture shock and a gradual loss of many traditional Balinese rights, wealth and local power. As the Balinese expressed their dilemma at that time, they were "as an egg being thrown against a rock."

Unfortunately for the Balinese, what remained of their fragile kingdom in 1906 was extremely vulnerable at a time when many of the world's great powers were politically willing to give tacit approval to what some historians called "manifest destiny." Such imperialistic moves were being sanctioned all over the world during what was to be the twilight years of international colonialism. Indeed, only 13 years earlier, another beautiful island kingdom, Hawaii, was overthrown by businessmen-revolutionaries backed up by U.S. military force. A few eyebrows were raised in Washington, but otherwise the Hawaiian *coup d'état* — like the one which followed in Bali — was simply regarded as a *fait accompli*. The pretext in Hawaii was to protect American sugar planters' business interests, whereas in Bali the Dutch operated on much flimsier legal grounds.

The Dutch had exercised strong control over the less attractive north side of Bali since as early as 1849 (following military campaigns in that region in 1846 and 1848), but the real jewel of the island, south-central Bali, had remained Balinese and fiercely independent, despite occasional conflicts between neighboring rajahdoms. By the turn of this century, the Dutch had made some political progress in the south (by forming alliances with the powerful rajahs of Ubud and Karangasem), but what they really wanted was complete control, so that all of Bali would be under the direct administration of the Netherlands Indies government. A military excuse to move on the south finally came, ironically, over a dispute between the Balinese and a Chinese shipping merchant from Borneo.

On May 27, 1904, a trading schooner, the *Sri Kumala*, ran onto a reef near the fishing village of Sanur. According to its Chinese owner, Balinese from nearby Badung and Gianyar boarded the *Sri Kumala* and exercised illegal salvage rights. He complained to the Dutch authorities, who in turn ordered the Rajah of Badung to pay the Chinese merchant a compensation of about 7,500 Dutch florins (then about 2,500 U.S. dollars). The Rajah simply refused to pay. Dickering between the Dutch and the Balinese continued for more than two years, until in June 1906, the Dutch finally acted on this small but convenient excuse to move militarily against the south of Bali. The Dutch first dispatched 12 warships to blockade the seacoasts off Badung and Tabanan, then waited and tried to negotiate for a few months. This made good diplomatic sense, but, as in the play recounted above, the Dutch simply received a big *tidak* (no) from the Rajah of Badung. On September 12, the Dutch General Ross Van Tonningen, commanding a Sixth Military Expedition fighting force of three infantry battalions, two artillery batteries and a cavalry detachment, delivered a final "do or die" ultimatum to the defiant Rajah. Again the warning was rejected, and two days later Dutch military forces began landing at Sanur Beach. After four days of slow, deliberate marching, the Dutch arrived at the royal palace (*puri*) of Badung-Denpasar. Except for the eerie beating of *kulkul* signal drums within the Rajah's palace-compound, the town was curiously deserted and silent. Then, as the Dutch closed in on the Denpasar-Badung *puri*, one of the great battlefield spectacles of modern times unfolded in front of their flabbergasted ranks.

"As they [the Dutch troops] drew closer," writes Willard A. Hanna in his book *Bali Profile*, "they observed a strange, silent procession emerging from the main gate of the *puri*." Then, as if in slow motion, a surrealistic movie played itself out in front of the startled Dutch. As Hanna describes events of that day:

It [the procession] was led by the Radja himself, seated in his state palanquin carried by four bearers, dressed in white cremation garments but splendidly bejeweled and armed with a magnificent kris. The Radja was followed by the officials of his court, the armed guards, the priests, his wives, his children, and his retainers, likewise

A Balineesche Schoone, or A Beauty of Bali, is the title of another fine portrait (right) taken by Ms. Weissenborn during one of her 1920s visits to Bali. This portrait and the one on page 42 were included in a special portfolio of Bali photographs published by Ms. Weissenborn's Lux Photo Studio, which was located in Garoet, Java.

dressed in white, flowers in their hair, many of them almost as richly ornamented and as splendidly armed as the Radja himself.

One hundred paces from the startled Dutch, the Radja halted his bearers, stepped from his palanquin, gave the signal, and the ghastly ceremony began. A priest plunged his dagger into the Radja's breast, and others of the company began turning their daggers upon themselves or upon one another … .

Other Balinese, however, ran amok and raced toward the Dutch soldiers, wildly flailing spears and krises. According to Dutch accounts, the Balinese attackers were crazed and in a state of trance. A command was given to open fire on the Balinese, and so Dutch cannons, gatling guns and small-arms fire literally tore the formally attired Balinese into pieces. As Hanna recounts, "Some of the (Balinese) women mockingly threw jewels and gold coins to the Dutch soldiers, and as more and more persons kept emerging from the palace gate, the mounds of corpses rose higher and higher."

In her important novel *A Tale From Bali*, the writer Vicki Baum, drawing from historical sources, recalled that not just men and women, but small boys and girls with flowers in their hair and young mothers with infants marched into the Dutch attack:

Hundreds fell to the enemy's rifles, hundreds more raised their krises high and plunged them into their breasts, plunging them in above the collar-bone so that the point should reach the heart in the ancient, holy way … Here and there, priests were to be seen among them, going calmly to and fro among the dying, and sprinkling holy water on their quivering bodies … .

As pitiful as this Balinese version of America's Wounded Knee or Trail of Tears was, the appalled Dutch Sixth Military Expedition had to grit its teeth and experience similar scenes later that same afternoon outside the nearby palaces of Pemetjutan and Tabanan, both due west of Badung. And two years later, on April 18, 1908, yet other Dutch soldiers watched helplessly, and in terrified awe, as the Dewa Agung of the Kingdom of Klungkung also chose to defend his home and honor in this grisly way. Some 200 Klungkung Balinese perished in that last *puputan*, including a half dozen of the Dewa Agung's wives, who ceremoniously knelt down beside his body and committed suicide by turning the kris on themselves after their husband had been killed by gunshot wounds. "Thus," writes Hanna, "on April 18, 1908, after 600 years of rule in Bali, the lineal descendants of the Madjapahit emperors were decimated, the ritualistic victims of relentless Western intrusion."

Meanwhile, the *Sri Kumala* captain was compensated for cargo losses, and the Dutch, in turn, claimed Bali.

When detailed accounts of these four *puputans* reached the outside world, international political pressure was brought to bear on the Dutch government and military, and from that time on, despite prevailing colonial policies, orders arrived from Amsterdam with demands that the Balinese were to be accorded "special" treatment. Colonial policies were reassessed and reformulated, a more benevolent breed of Dutch administrators were dispatched to Bali, and the island was officially recognized as a, well, "different" and "fragile" political, cultural and economic entity, distinct from Java and other colonial holdings of the Netherlands Indies.

Indeed, the previously imperious Dutch went out of their way to atone for past sins. New medical clinics and schools were built, an island-wide network of roads and bridges was engineered, important buildings (including temples and palaces) were restored, and communications facilities were established to put the long-isolated island in touch with the world beyond its shores. And except for the abolishment of traditional Balinese practices such as *suttee* (widow-burning) and slavery, a concerted effort was made to revive and encourage Balinese cultural pursuits. Another positive Dutch contribution was the establishment of a proper legal system, complete with a Balinese-style court, or *Kerta*, that did its best to mete out justice fairly and without prejudicial treatment based on one's religious preferences or caste distinction.

One policy that drew snickers from abroad, however, involved Dutch attempts to impose modesty on the Balinese by ordering traditionally topless Balinese women to cover their breasts when in the presence of foreigners. Visiting missionaries and strait-laced colonial administrators were concerned that the sight

Three formal studies of high caste Balinese entitled Children of the King of Bali (right), The King of Bali, ca. 1875, *and* Baliers (following pages) *were taken in Bali by photographers from a Jakarta-based photo studio called Woodbury & Page. This British photographic firm operated in Jakarta, or Batavia, from 1870 to 1890.*

of bare-breasted Balinese maidens here and there in public view would incite randy Dutch soldiers and other males unaccustomed to such nudity to think sinful thoughts and sexually exploit the native women. The Balinese, of course, merely laughed at such notions and returned to life as normal.

But to their credit, given the fragmented conditions of Bali's society, the Dutch also strictly and paternalistically regulated the comings, goings and many varied schemes being promoted by the many and assorted entrepreneurs, missionaries and outright scam-artists who invariably flock to such places for an easy life and quick money. Extremely strict travel restrictions were imposed on such outsiders, making it difficult for all but the most enterprising of their ilk to visit — and cash in — on this new Eden just eight degrees south of the equator.

The occupying Dutch, however, were not entirely altruistic. If there was money to be made on the island of Bali, the Dutch made it, even if the product that was going to be sold for profit was of a dubious nature. The greatest source of Dutch income on Bali during the decade following the *puputan*, for example, was opium, that insidious commodity that the British had exploited so efficiently in China. Opium had long been a great source of wealth to the Balinese Rajahs who for many decades had controlled its distribution on the island, and though the Dutch well knew how dangerous this drug was to any society, they decided to make the most of the by then well-addicted and captive Balinese opium market. Instead of outlawing the drug they opted to regulate it. Or as Hanna writes, "While earnestly advising the Radjas and the people against its use, they promulgated the *opiumregie* which had already afforded them great moral and financial comfort in Java." This *opiumregie*, which officially went into effect on January 1, 1908, allowed anybody on the island over the age of 18 to legally purchase opium at one of 100 official sales outlets strictly controlled by the Dutch suppliers and authorities.

The opium monopoly on Bali proved to be extremely profitable. Net profit on sales of this drug, according to Hanna, was about 90 per cent of its import cost to the Dutch, so as early as 1909, only one year after the Dutch had instituted the opium monopoly, sales of opium accounted "for about 75 per cent of the administrative budget and assured the [Dutch] Re-

sidency each year of a very gratifying surplus which was often larger than total expenditure."

Unfortunately, as was the case in other Dutch colonial holdings of that time, little of the money made in this nefarious way ever trickled down to the Balinese. In the year 1910, for example, Hanna cites figures which show that though "the Dutch realized well over 1,000,000 Dutch florins from the sale of opium in Bali, they expended less than 20,000 Dutch florins on schools, increasing their educational budget only very modestly and gradually thereafter."

Once they were comfortably ensconced in power, and enjoying a positive cash flow from the island's resources, the Dutch tried to "hollandize" Bali as much as possible. Most of their influence has been muted or eroded during the years following World War II, but now and then you can still spot quaint Batavia-style remnants of the Netherlands Indies on Bali. Drive through the cooler highlands above Singaraja or through some of the older suburbs of Denpasar and you will see many still standing examples of Dutch architecture in the form of steepled and double-doored homes, wrought-iron gate and grill details and, most commonly, wrought-iron and porcelain Dutch hanging lamps. Perhaps the best lingering reminder of this period, however, is the old Bali Hotel in Denpasar (now the Bali Natour Hotel), which used to cater to early visitors who would arrive in Bali by K. P. M. Dutch steamship at Singaraja and then motor across the scenic island to Denpasar. History has altered the look of this place, and Bali is no longer the "Young Holland" the Dutch once hoped it would become, but all of the above are fascinating reminders of the island's turbulent and fickle colonial past.

Though Holland's official, hands-off policy is often credited with not just preserving what was left of things Balinese, but also with encouraging an efflorescence, or renaissance, of culture on the island, the Dutch soon found it was difficult to keep a bureaucratic lid on this Fantasyland called Bali. Very soon after political matters had settled down, a number of books, magazine articles and other media began paying special attention to the island. Reports began filtering back to Europe and the Americas that the newly "discovered" and accessible island of Bali, not Hawaii, Tahiti or the Virgin islands, was *the* Last Paradise on Earth and *the* chic place to visit in this part of the world.

Idyllic streamside scenes such as this one (right) were popularly reproduced in books about Bali which were published for general overseas consumption during the first half of this century. Many of these books were of questionable artistic and literary taste, but each further perpetuated the "Bali as Paradise" myth.

These proud Dutch troopers, members of the Koninliske Nederlands Indisch Leger (the Royal
Dutch Indies Army), were photographed on Bali during the time of the 1906 puputan
massacres. The KNIL, or "Jantjes" (Little Johns) as they were called, are pictured with some of
the weapons they used against the Balinese during their bloody battles at Denpasar,
Pemetjutan, Tabanan and later (in 1908) at Klungkung.

The first night on shore [September 15, 1906] passed quietly, but day had scarcely broken when the Balinese attempted to attack the [Dutch invasion force's] camp. The poor fellows retreated hopelessly when their lances and bravery came face to face with our modern weapons. Their plan had been to attack in the night but the blinding searchlights of the warships that had lit up the entire beach had defeated and paralyzed them. During the next days there was no cease in the dull drone of cannon fire from the warships. As safe as they would be at shooting practice home with mother, the *Jantjes* loaded and shot their guns at an invisible enemy in the equally invisible Den Pasar. With each shot I felt pain at the thought that one of those giant shells might explode on a living compound and spread agony by flattening some house. Thankfully, the target was distant and its precise location not known ... After Sanur, the surrounding desas of Renong, Panjar and Sesetan were also captured ...

— *from an eyewitness account of the Badung puputan, 1906, by the Dutch artist-adventurer W. O. J. Nieuwenkamp. From Zwerftochten Op Bali (Wanderings in Bali), 1910, by Nieuwenkamp. Translation by Bruce Carpenter.*

'PARADISE'
As Seen Through a Lens

PHOTOGRAPHY — THAT BLINKING ART - SCIENCE that first fixes a single image on the silver-salted emulsion of light-sensitive paper, and then magically transfers that image to the emulsion of a viewer's mind — probably has had more to do with the spread of popular and romantic myths about Bali than any other medium. Because the island of Bali was for some 300 years only one obscure dot in the vast, largely unexplored Indonesian archipelago, early pictures of this fascinating but

remote island were rare. European photo archives include fine daguerreotypes, ambrotypes and other early examples of photography that were captured by travelers while on visits to larger Indonesian islands such as Java, Sumatra and Borneo, but for perhaps a half century following the development of photography (in the mid-to-late 1800s), Bali was all but bypassed by the first serious travel photographers in this part of the world. Just after 1900, however, stories about the Dutch East Indies government's military campaigns against Bali began inspiring photographers to drop by and take long, lingering looks at the island through their camera lenses.

The first of these photographers were usually documentary cameramen who joined Dutch colonial officials on approved propaganda tours of the island. These camera-toting civil servants invariably set up perfunctory portraits of high-ranking Balinese officials, sweeping studies of curious architectural and archaeological sites, and, of course, public relations photographs of stiff Dutch administrators earnestly at work and at play in Holland's newest colonial acquisition. Unfortunately, most of those first photographs were published only in Holland, and usually as a part of back chapters in tedious and poorly circulated government journals about Indonesia.

Just before the onset of World War I, however, a traveling German doctor who was also quite a keen and sensitive amateur photographer was assigned by Dutch civil authorities to help provide medical services at a clinic that had been established in the highland village of Bangli in central Bali. That physician-photographer, Gregor Krause, arrived in Bali intent on practicing medicine, but what he did in his spare time, during the years 1912 to 1914, was also to travel

throughout the island with a hefty viewfinder camera and a large supply of photographic plates. Krause focused his bulky camera's sights on landscapes, seascapes, temple festivals, artworks, architecture and nearly everything of human interest. Photography was a tedious, unwieldy and time-consuming process in those days, particularly in the tropics where it required extreme care and patience, but during his two years on the island of Bali, Dr. Krause found time to make some 4,000 photographic exposures of Balinese people, places and things. His forté was people, and when it came to people he was particularly fond of photographing them in various states of undress. The nude body, male or female, preoccupied the bulk of his work on Bali.

"Who has created these bodies and conducts their perfect movements?" he asked in a first book of his Bali photographs that was published in Holland in 1922. "Indeed," he wrote, "the Balinese seem to be chiseled out of basalt. Nothing about their bodies is coarse, clumsy or awkward; every limb, every posture, every movement, is noble and graceful. They have velvet skin which shares the delicate slenderness and strength of the skeleton."

Following his productive two-year sojourn in Bali, Dr. Krause was transferred to a medical post in Borneo (where he curiously produced two portfolios of photographs of monkeys). But before he left Bali, he arranged for his thousands of photographs to be shipped to a publisher friend in Holland named Karl With. With Krause's consent, With put together a collection of introductory Bali essays — separately authored by Krause, With and an etymologist named Ernst Furhrmann — and produced a hefty photo-book, *Insel Bali*, which was released by the Dutch publishing

Gregor Krause's sensual photographs of Balinese people (left and above) firmly established Bali as a paradisiacal land unlike no other on earth, and when significant numbers of travelers began visiting the island, the Balinese graciously lived up to their most exotic expectations. Bali, not Tahiti, Jamaica or other such islands, soon became the number one island in the world to visit.

house Folkwang Verlag G.M.B.H., The Hague, in 1922. This 176-page book, first published in German and later in an abbreviated French edition, was such a publishing success that its first printing was sold out within six months. During the next few years it was republished in various forms, but most notably in a German edition entitled *Bali: Volk, Land, Tanze, Feste, Temple* (*Bali: People, the Land, Dances, Festivals, Temples*). The most popular edition of this book was released worldwide from Munich in 1926.

By then, Krause was back in Europe, being celebrated in literary and art salons as *the* photographer "who has given birth to a new vision of Paradise." Indeed, German photographer Krause's Bali photographs were to the Indonesian island of Bali what the French artist Paul Gauguin's paintings had been to the Polynesian island of Tahiti some 30 years earlier. Appropriately, the first major Dutch exhibition of Krause's Bali photographs was sponsored and organized in Europe by the traveler cum artist W.O.J. Nieuwenkamp, whose extensive work on behalf of Bali is discussed in a following chapter on art in Bali.

Krause's romantic (some said "lurid") photographs and rambling, metaphysical prose became all the rage in a Europe where post-Victorian industrialization and the bloody First World War had muted dreams of Eden-like islands. In his books, he breathed new life into old ideas about tropical idylls populated by serene and noble savages. Predictably, he inspired yet other photographers and journalists to visit that unreal place, Bali, "where an archetypal environment with genuine evaluation codes and an intact social life is rooted in the close and undisturbed contact of its inhabitants to nature."

"People nowadays have almost lost their sense for unity in life; the umbilical cord between heaven, God and earth has been torn," Krause and With wrote. But on the island of Bali, they said, "this unity is still intact." Bored European and American intellectuals read these words, their eyes glazed over, and they very soon found themselves boarding steamships bound for the world's newest and perhaps Last Paradise.

Even the visiting artist-author Miguel Covarrubias credits photographer Krause as being the inspiration for his visiting and working on Bali. In the introduction to his book *Island of Bali* he writes that he and his wife, Rose, "had seen a splendid album of Bali photographs (*Bali*, by Gregor Krause), and gradually we had developed an irresistible desire to see the island, until one spring day of 1930 we found ourselves, rather unexpectedly, on board the *Cingalese Prince*, a freighter bound for the Dutch East Indies." Once on Bali, the Covarrubiases found even more of what Krause had photographed, and their subsequent book, first published in 1937 by Alfred A Knopf, Inc. (with a 60-page album of some 140 more photographs by Rose Covarrubias), attracted even more Paradise-seekers to Bali.

During the period between Krause's visit and World War II (when the island was effectively shut down for four years by the Japanese occupation of Indonesia), scores of other, equally romantic books about Bali were published. Some were serious studies of the island and its vibrant culture, but most of them were poorly written and profusely illustrated with portraits of stately, bare-breasted women. Cultural activities were almost an afterthought in many of these sensationalized publications. The Bali myth continued to spread, however, and fast on the heels of these first still photographers also came even more artists, photographers, writers, and, beginning in 1926, cinematographers. By 1932 even glitzy Hollywood got into the Bali act when a tantalizing movie about Bali was produced and widely circulated by the American filmmakers André Roosevelt and Armand Denis. The title of that movie, *Goona, Goona, An Authentic Melodrama*, became a popular byword for tropical sensuality, and Bali's highly eroticized pull became even stronger.

Indeed, how could anyone resist the siren call of Bali after reading in Hickman Powell's *The Last Paradise* (1930) about "a solitary female figure, swinging toward us up the road" whose "maiden breasts projected angular, living shadows" that "embodied dreams of pastoral poets." In this woman's eyes, gushed Powell, "burned the afterglow of fallen empires."

In his official autobiography (*Charles Chaplin, My Autobiography*) published in 1964 by the Bodley Head, London, the movie star Charlie Chaplin summed up Bali's hedonistic appeal during the 1930s in this way: "It was Sydney [Chaplin's brother] who had recommended visiting the island of Bali, saying how untouched it was by civilization and describing its beautiful women with their exposed bosoms. These," he wrote with a wink, "aroused my interest."

The German artist-adventurer Walter Spies was also handy with a camera, as evidenced by this action shot captured during a particularly aggressive barong dance. Spies' heavily retouched photograph, which shows a barong lion attacking his nemesis, the witch-goddess Rangda, first appeared in a 1930s travel book commissioned by Holland's KPM shipping line.

Since the mid 1930s, one of the most popular tourist attractions on Bali has been the animated, a cappella kecak dance, also commonly called the "monkey dance." This particular kecak group, photographer unknown, was caught in action at the village of Bona in Gianyar province, ca. 1936. A detail of the bottom photo appears as this book's frontispiece.

Henri Cartier-Bresson, the eminent French photographer who
specializes in black-and-white photography, visited Bali in 1954, and
while on the island he captured many fine and ironic images of
Balinese life and religious rituals. The shots on these pages were
taken at a barong dance ritual, during which possessed devotees fall
into varied states of trance and attack themselves with krises.

The late German photographer Ernst Haas, who was in Bali at the same time as Cartier-Bresson (preceding pages), attended a village janger youth dance concert and produced this shot. Three female janger dancers await their turn to dance while framed by the swaying hands and bodies of their male counterparts.

Photographer Helmi (see page 64) identified the action in this
unusual photograph as a "War of the [Leftover] Offerings," or, in
Indonesian, "Perang Sampian." During this rite, men of the village of
Samuan Tiga reenact a peace celebration which took place in ancient
times when three Balinese kingdoms stopped warring with each other.

French photographer Bruno Barbey, a member of Paris' prestigious Magnum Photo Agency, took these photographs of religious rites in Ubud in 1979 during the month of January. Villagers place offerings at a shrine inside a green jungle vale at Campuan (above), and, a few days later, a throng of thousands surround the grand cremation badé (right) of Ubud's late king, the Tjokorda Gde Agung Sukawati.

Japanese photographer Hiroshi Suga has recently produced two
books about Bali which have been very well received in his home
country. Two studies taken during recent visits to the island feature
banten-*carrying women* (left) *during a Balinese festival period and a
group of purple-hatted* baris gede *warrior dancers* (above).

A COUNTRY STUDIO
In Black Velvet and Bamboo

O BSERVED THROUGH A CAMERA LENS, BALI offers the photographer — whether amateur or professional — some of the richest visual material to be found anywhere in the world. Stunning amber-emerald rice terraces, azure blue seascapes and religious festivals ablaze with color are found, usually unexpectedly, at nearly every turn in a country road. During my many photo shoots on the island, I have invariably found myself scurrying for fresh supplies of film, reloading like mad, then

rushing back to frame an apparition that has just stumbled into view. Because Bali is so graphic, the sheer volume and diversity of photographic subjects can be overwhelming. Consider what begins as a simple portrait of a young village girl. As I move in to photograph her, the picture becomes pleasantly complicated as friends and relatives gather around, all of them laughing and wanting to be included in the picture. Later, as I step back and change to a wide-angle lens, I feel compelled to enhance the frame by including a stand of wonderfully backlit palm trees (and, of course, a temple spire or two). A simple portrait thus unexpectedly became a panorama of the girl's village.

I found that the only way I could successfully isolate a single subject in such a social setting was to "neutralize" the background, or, in effect, to create a portable and easily mobile studio. This isn't a new idea (indeed, many of the world's first traveling photographers set up pictures this way), but I was keen to work in Bali with a team of assistants and a somewhat primitive assemblage of light tents and bamboo scaffolding hacked out of a local jungle. The idea of building such a portable studio, then inviting the local populace to pay a visit, was intriguing.

My first step was to visit the chaotic cloth market near the central market in Denpasar town. Once there, I found myself haggling in broken Indonesian for two three-meter lengths of what a salesman called "bleu druze," or black velvet. This process took the better part of a morning as I compared prices in various shops, bargained aggresively, then waited for a tailor to sew the velvet lengths together into a studio backdrop. Later, at my first shooting site in the village of Batuan, I watched and directed as the velvet backdrop was attached to a bamboo pole, suspended by rope between two thatched huts, then brushed clean by village boys using grass brooms. Next came the subjects, and for openers I selected and photographed some of Batuan's most renowned painters, puppeteers, dancers and musicians.

Eventually, as I moved from one field location to another, I found myself drawn more and more to ordinary, everyday people who just happened to pass by. Here comes a man in blue sunglasses out for a walk with his haughty cockerel. There goes a housewife with a huge storage tin balanced on her head. A few moments later they too were posing like professionals in front of the black velvet suspended beneath bamboo.

Lighting was never easy because I constantly had to dismantle the studio and reassemble it as the sun traveled in an arc across the equatorial sky. I learned very quickly, however, that backlighting seemed to produce the effect I most wanted. It was the closest thing I could see to what painters refer to as a soft north light. In order to fill in foreground shadows, I had village boys hold up reflectors made of white paper mounted onto wood panels. Occasionally, because of weather or other circumstances, I had to shoot indoors. At those times I used two portable flash units in silver studio umbrellas to create the same effect.

The final results were surprising. Professional photographers are not supposed to be surprised by their results, but I was, and pleasantly so. In the end, though, I must applaud the Balinese people, who graciously participated in this experiment and presented themselves and their images in many unusual, compelling and creative ways.

— R. Ian Lloyd

Photographer Lloyd, who took most of this book's photographs, is shown at work (above) with his portable, black velvet studio set up in the village of Batuan. Curious children gather round as he takes a flashlight meter reading of a young legong dancer who had been dressed and made up especially for this unusual photo opportunity.

Three principal dancers of a legong keraton *ensemble strike stylized dance positions. The center dancer, known as the* condong, *is the fiery gypsy of the group, and the matched pair of legongs behind her are her attendants. These three characters dance out an episode, from the* Malat, *a story based on the Balinese* Thousand and One Nights. *The* legong *is arguably Bali's finest dance form.*

These mustached boys in red headbands (above) sway through the sinuous moves of a folk dance called the gopala. The gopala was choreographed in recent years in honor of Bali's cowherds. Another *"modern"* dance is the kebyar duduk (right). Kebyar dances were first composed and performed in the 1930s and made internationally famous by the dancer I Mario, a native of Tabanan.

The neighing steed (at stage left) *is a member of a classical gambuh operatic troupe from the village of Batuan. Gambuh is one of Bali's oldest dance forms. It is constantly being modernized, although it takes most of its themes from 14th century Majapahit court stories. Striking a similarly bemused pose* (above) *is Batuan's Wayan Supir.*

Set up a country studio and you will soon find the most enthusiastic models mugging in front of your backdrop. On this particular day of shooting, a village woman bearing a container made of biscuit tins (left) passes by, flashing a smile. Next on the scene is a painter, Dewa Kandel (above), who happened by while taking his handsome white fighting cock out for a leisurely afternoon stroll.

The proud chaps on these two pages are gambuh actors who have
been cast in the roles of first minister (left) and second minister
(above) to a grand rajah of Majapahit. Their opulent headgear,
shoulder capes and face paintings indicate their courtly rank.

Male and female dancers of a janger dance troupe (above and right)
take a break between performances to sit and stand for formal group
portraits. The janger is a popular, coed dance style that was
developed in about 1925 and has been enthusiastically enjoyed ever
since. According to some sources it was inspired by the dancing of
visiting Malay operetta groups that had toured in Bali.

The prancing feet, flickering fingers and animated eyes (at left)
belong to a young solo baris dancer. The baris dance, commonly
referred to as the warrior-drill dance, is performed in solo and group
styles throughout Bali. Enjoying the baris action (above) is Wayan
Narta, a well-known dalang, or shadow puppet master, from Sukawati.

One of the most animated and entertaining of all Balinese dance forms is the classical topeng, or masked dance. In this particular sequence (left and above), a topeng dancer, Wayan Regug, is shown preparing for the role of a comical female character known as "the coquette." This character is extremely ugly, but she is convinced that she is beautiful and eminently attractive to all men.

Wayan Regug, the fellow who treated us to a quick-change demonstration on the previous pages, here exhibits some of the many faces of a typical topeng dancer-actor including those of a king, priests, noblemen, clowns and, once again, the beautiful but ugly coquette. *Following pages: Six little Balinese girls pose in formal dance costume before performing a traditional pendet dance.*

W. O. J. NIEUWENKAMP *(1874–1950)*
Bangli, pencil and ink on paper,
original size unknown, 1918

A RENAISSANCE
In Ways of Seeing Things

SHORTLY AFTER THE ARRIVAL AND INSTALLAtion of Dutch conquerors in south Bali in 1906, nearly all of the traditional arts of Bali, including music, dance, sculpture and Kamasan-style painting, entered a period of creative neglect. Normal religious and secular lifecycle rituals were observed, but when it came to fine arts activities, the Balinese were understandably cowed and too busy adjusting psychologically to a new colonial government and to what pop anthropologists call

"culture shock". In the wake of all this social-political-cultural turmoil, however, scores of "modern" ideas and conveniences were introduced into Bali — in the form of international communications, combustion engines, electricity, much-needed medical care — and, for better or worse, what we now condescendingly call tourists.

These latter-day creatures, lured to Bali by the occasional stories and pictures that sang the praises of an unspoiled tropical paradise, were not too unlike most travelers today. They did not have to worry about jet-lag, computer breakdowns, body and film scanners and other inconveniences of the current aerospace age, but instead had to endure the then rampant malaria, suspect foods and long, monotonous cruises on hot cargo ships by way of exotic tropical ports such as Singapore, Macassar, Padang, Batavia, and Surabaya before reaching Bali.

Historian Willard A. Hanna, in his *Bali Profile — People, Events, Circumstances, 1001–1976*, reports that initially the protective Dutch "entertained grave misgivings" about the effects that tourism would have upon Bali and the Balinese, so for many years the colonial Residency went out of its way to "shelter the island from world travelers." The Dutch authorities "undertook also to shelter the travelers from exposure to what might be the irresistible temptation to settle in and to stay, perhaps to corrupt, or to be corrupted by, the presumably innocent but hedonistic Balinese."

This policy was at first generally successful in containing the activities of aggressive missionaries, merchants and tourists, but, as Hanna writes, "foreign anthropologists, archaeologists, ethnologists, artists, musicians, dancers, and actors, and eventually sociologists, economists, and political scientists of more or less reputable professional credentials, not to mention numerous drifters and the occasional diplomats, inevitably and eagerly sought out Bali on missions at times indistinguishable from tourism." As it holds true today, so did it then: where there was a strong will to stay on in Bali, there always was a way, whatever the official or academically esoteric excuse.

One fascinating chap who was favored by the Dutch both before and during those early years of colonial occupation was a fine artist and more than serious traveler by the name of W.O.J. Nieuwenkamp (1874–1950). The son of an Amsterdam shipping agent, Nieuwenkamp had at a very young age left Holland to become a wanderer. During his youth he had been trained in art at the Amsterdam Art Academy, and he supported himself in his travels — first in Europe and later in Asia — by selling his original artworks and by writing and illustrating articles for various Dutch magazines and newspapers.

Eventually, in 1898, at the age of 24, Nieuwenkamp journeyed to the Dutch East Indies and fell in love with the vast and exotic Indonesian archipelago. He returned to Holland that same year, but in 1904 wanderlust again struck and so he made a second trip to Indonesia. This time he visited Bali, where he produced the first of many sketches and field notes that eventually were published as a book, *Bali en Lombok*. It was the first and is still one of the finest illustrated guides to Bali. "There is so much beauty to be seen and sketched here that has never been appreciated or spoken of before. For that reason I have decided to make an illustrated book on Bali, the most wonderful land that I know," Nieuwenkamp wrote in 1904.

Bruce Carpenter, an American film-maker and multi-media artist who has authored an as yet unpublished biography of Nieuwenkamp, wrote recently

Two Bali studies by the Dutch artist W. O. J. Nieuwenkamp (left and above) open a special portfolio of artworks created during the past century by non-Balinese artists. Nieuwenkamp's works are reproduced here by courtesy of the Nieuwenkamp family. Other paintings in this portfolio are reproduced by courtesy of the Neka Museum, Campuan-Ubud, unless otherwise credited.

that Nieuwenkamp fell so in love with Bali that he "set out to work immediately with a burning passion — drawing, traveling, asking questions, recording answers and learning native ways and crafts. Pushing himself to his physical limits, he was forced to stop and return to Holland only after suffering several long bouts of severe malarial fevers. In spite of the illness he was overjoyed, for with him he carried a large portfolio of sketches, the first illustrations ever made by an occidental [on site] on Bali. He was convinced that he would hereby demonstrate to the Dutch public and artists their folly in ignoring this and other precious gems in their far-flung colonial empire."

Following a second visit to Bali, over a period of several months during 1906-1907, Nieuwenkamp produced what Carpenter calls "the first illustrated book on Bali and Balinese art" and "also one of the first attempts to present the people, their island and culture as a whole." This was a book appropriately entitled *Zwerftochten op Bali*, or *Wanderings in Bali*.

In the preface to this landmark book, published in 1910 by the Dutch house of Elseviers, Nieuwenkamp wondered aloud that, "How peculiar that among our large body of colonial literature dated before 1900, that there is not one of those many thousands of books and articles that speaks of Balinese Art [even though] Bali has been known to us for more than three hundred years." During the process of preparing final sketches and paintings for this book, Nieuwenkamp pedaled about Bali alone on a bicycle and produced not just fine landscapes, seascapes, portraits and architectural studies, but also the first detailed drawings and descriptions of the famed Moon of Pejeng kettle-gong and the complex double-*ikat* weaving works of the village of Tenganan called *geringsing*. He was also a witness, coincidentally, of the spectacular 1906 Badung (Denpasar) *puputan* massacre, and his vivid descriptions of day-to-day events of that military expedition are of great historical importance.

Nieuwenkamp's artistic studies and writings attracted great interest in Europe when they were exhibited and published, and, in turn, they inspired yet other writers, artists and scholars to visit Bali.

One fine artist who may have been drawn to Bali by Nieuwenkamp's early works was a Moscow-born German by the name of Walter Spies. There is no direct evidence linking Spies to Nieuwenkamp, but it is interesting to note that in 1924 a widely-publicized retrospective exhibition of Nieuwenkamp's Indonesia work was held at the Gallery Kleykamp in The Hague on the occasion of the latter's 50th birthday. This event is mentioned because it is coincidental that the Gallery Kleykamp also exhibited, within one year of the Nieuwenkamp retrospective, a collection of paintings by Spies. "It would seem strange," writes Carpenter, "if Spies did not see something of Nieuwenkamp's work, which might have been his first introduction to Bali."

Whatever Nieuwenkamp's influence, historians do know that only a year later, the then 28-year-old Spies impulsively left Europe for Indonesia, where he first took up work as the director-conductor of a European orchestra maintained by the Sultan of Yogyakarta in Central Java. During his first year in Java, Spies visited Bali, fell in love with what he saw, and vowed to return.

In mid-1927, Spies gave up his job in Yogya and took up residence in the *puri* (palace) of the Sukawatis, the ruling family of the Balinese village of Ubud. While in Ubud, a cool, rice-growing retreat in south-central Bali, Spies continued to indulge his passion for music, but he also used the quiet time he found there to practice his second love, sketching and painting. During the next 13 years, Spies produced a series of fanciful, sometimes surrealistic oil paintings that were technically superb. He didn't paint very many pictures, but those that he did complete were usually bought up by resident or visiting Europeans who appreciated his contemporary painting style.

The work Spies was doing in Bali was very personal, but his earnest artistic activity soon attracted the attention of local *Kamasan*-style artisans who lived in Ubud and other neighboring *desas*. These traditional *wayang* painters would visit Spies in his small home-studio in Campuan-Ubud, and while there they avidly studied his drawing and painting techniques. Eventually they left the side of their German guru and tried their hand at Western-style art. What resulted was a new and uniquely Balinese form of modern art that has since become established as an artistic genre.

Spies' influence was formidable, but as other European and American artists began arriving on Bali, the Balinese learned even more. Especially influential after Spies was the Dutch artist Rudolf Bonnet (1895-1978), who taught the Balinese classical art disciplines he had mastered in art academies in Holland and Italy.

RUDOLF BONNET *(1895–1978)*
Ardjuna Wiwaha, tempera and crayon on paper
(H×W: 88×74 cm) 1953

Walter Spies (1895–1942) was a young musician-artist-drifter who found in Bali a vision of paradise he could only dream of in post-war industrial Europe. Influenced in part by Rousseau, and inspired by the Balinese lifestyle and landscape, he settled into the island like a bird in a nest. He learned Bali's language and arts, and soon became *the man* to see when you were in Bali and wanted to know what was happening. During the years he lived there (1927–1938), his bamboo, wood and thatch home in Campuan-Ubud became a busy salon abuzz with curious foreigners, many of whom were visiting artists, intellectuals and film stars.

Throughout those Bali years, however, Spies indulged a personal fondness for young Balinese boys, and this proclivity to forbidden fruit — coupled with the fact that he was born a German eventually led to his banishment from Eden. As World War II began looming on distant East and West horizons, conservative and suspicious Dutch administrators ordered Spies to be taken into custody (on December 31, 1938) on criminal charges of moral turpitude. Overnight, Spies' dream of an island became a nightmare of incarceration — first in a Denpasar jail, then in prisons at Surabaya and Ngawi in Java and, eventually, at Kotatjane in North Sumatra. On January 18, 1942, Spies and some 1,500 other German civilians who had been interned in Dutch East Indies prisons were transferred to three Dutch ships bound for India and Ceylon from Padang in Sumatra. Two vessels reached their destinations, but the third one, the *Van Imhoff*, did not. On the *Van Imhoff's* second day at sea, she was hit by a Japanese aerial bomb. Among the casualties who died on that ship was the dreamer Spies.

WALTER SPIES *(1895–1942)*
Die Landschaft und ihre Kinder, *oil on board*
(H×W: 62×91 cm), 1939
From the Hans Rhodius Collection
By courtesy of the Walter Spies Foundation, Holland

Dutch artist Arie Smit has lived in various parts of Bali since 1956, moving from one part of the island to another when wanderlust strikes. He has been in Indonesia since 1938, first working in Java as a Dutch army lithographer. He is particularly known for his studies of and encouragement of a naive Balinese painting form popularly known as the "Young Artists" style.

ARIE SMIT *(1916–   )*
Pemuda Bali (Balinese Youth), *oil on canvas*
(H×W: 80×80 cm), 1981

Han Snel came to Indonesia as a Dutch conscript soldier in 1946, but then chose to become a naturalized Indonesian citizen in 1950, the year he moved to Bali. His home is in Ubud. Snel calls his abstract painting style "roundism." In this portrait, Snel poses with some of his paintings. Obliging as human easels are his Balinese wife Ne Madé Siti (to his right), four of their children, and friends.

HAN SNEL *(1925–   )*
Gadis-gadis Menjunjung Sesajen (Girls Carrying Offerings),
oil on canvas, (H×W: 70×50 cm), 1976

Antonio Maria Blanco who was born in Manila is an animated
Spaniard of Catalan ancestry. He has traveled widely and arrived in
Bali to stay and paint in 1952. He lives atop a hill in Campuan-Ubud
with his wife, Ni Ronji, who has borne him three daughters and a son.
Senor and Senora Blanco pose in his studio (above) with eight
self-portraits created by Senor Blanco.

ANTONIO MARIA BLANCO *(1926–   )*
Wanita Eve dan buah apel (Eve With an Apple),
water color on paper, (H×W: 67×78 cm), 1973

MIGUEL COVARRUBIAS *(1904—1957)*
A Balinese Girl Carrying Rice on Her Head,
watercolor on paper, (H×W: 35×25 cm), 1930

WILLEM G. HOFKER *(1902–1981)*
Ni Gusti Nyoman Kelepon, Arja Dancer,
crayon on paper, (H×W: 47×29 cm), 1943

DONALD FRIEND *(1915–   )*
Batu Jimbar, *gouache and acrylic on paper,*
(H×W: 48×64 cm), 1976

THEO MEIER *(1908–1982)*
Two Balinese Girls in the Flower Garden,
oil on canvas, (H×W: 110×78 cm), 1979

AFFANDI *(1907–   )*
Perahu Nelayan Bali (Balinese Fishing Boats),
oil on canvas, (H×W: 103×129 cm), 1975

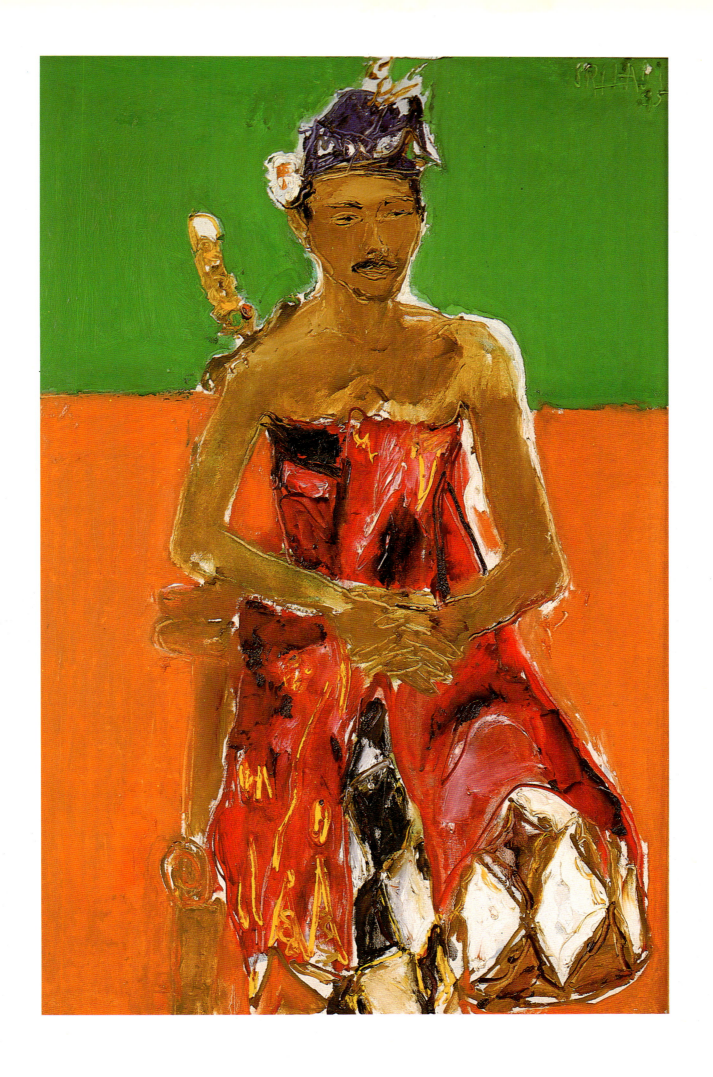

SRIHADI *(1931–   )*
Suteja Neka, oil on canvas,
(H×W: 141×92 cm), 1975

ART
Offerings of the Soul

AS YOU ZIG-ZAG YOUR WAY THROUGH THE MAIN streets of Denpasar, the back roads of Karangasem, or even the temple-dotted rice fields of coastal Tabanan, pause for a moment and study the many sculptures, temple cloths and animated bas reliefs that embellish ceremonial structures, backyard shrines and even the walls of Kuta Beach's Kentucky Fried Chicken outlet. Now, close your eyes and think of Walt Disney, "Star Wars" and Hollywood. Imagine all those grimacing, smirking and

posturing demons, deities and beauties of Bali in dancing, full-color animation on the screen of your neighborhood theater, or inside that magical living-room box we call a television. In the next creative step, take pen and paper in hand, and with all the imagination you can conjure, tell a story. Any kind of story. Funny or sad. Classical or mundane. War and peace. Indeed, let the muse fly, and once your film script and story-boards are complete, take the whole works to a big Hollywood producer or director who is on the lookout for newly creative talent.

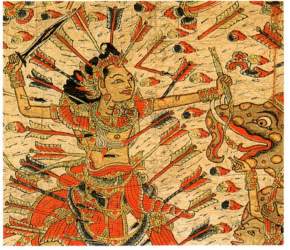

That is apparently what early Balinese sketch artists did, but instead of deriving inspiration from an electronic box or motion picture screen, they were moved to artistic expression by the flickering movements of a magic lantern show called *wayang kulit*, or shadow puppet theater, which was imported here more than a thousand years ago from India by way of Java, India, Thailand and other Asian countries.

Not unlike the modern Balinese who now sit in their village *banjar*, mouths agape during a televised rerun of "Hawaii Five-O" or BBC footage of a coup attempt in Thailand, the Balinese used to squat in front of a stretched cloth screen and marvel at tales from the *Mahabharata* and *Ramayana* epics of India as they were interpreted by a visiting *dalang*, or puppet master, who simultaneously acted as storyteller, religion proselytizer, priest, disc jockey, musical conductor and lighting technician. From his big wooden box full of leather puppets came principal actors, supporting actors and, to use an old Cecil B. deMille phrase, "a cast of thousands." It has been a long time since the first *dalang* arrived here, set up a screen and projection lamp, and began wowing the locals with stories about faraway

places and times, but to this day that early "cinematic" art form continues to inform and inspire enthusiastic Bali locals into a pleasantly suspended state of disbelief. Indeed, *wayang kulit* was to old Bali what televisions and movies are to Los Angeles, Paris or Tokyo today. It was a medium that communicated ancient truths through the use of a new and animated lie.

Foreign and local art historians tend to agree that the first and most influential graphic design artists in Bali were probably the practicing *dalang* who carefully carved and painted their leather puppets to create a greater spiritual mystique and generate what we now call "audience appeal." In their wooden boxes full of *wayang kulit* (literally "skin shadows") were the precursors of the images you now see in Bali's sacred palm-leaf books (*lontar*), in the relief images that work and play on the walls of the island's many temples and courtyards, and — in a blown-up, three-dimensional way — as standing wood and stone sculptures (sword-bearing guardians, soaring Garuda birds or water-bearing nymphs) that appear here and there in public and private places throughout the island of Bali.

Before visiting foreign artists began arriving in Bali during the early part of this century, nearly all graphic art extant on Bali was rendered in simple and earthy colors and forms that were derived from or influenced by *wayang* puppetry. This "classical" style of Balinese-Hindu iconography was most actively practiced, according to most sources, in the village of Kamasan in the ancient kingdom of Gelgel. There, paintings were used early on to decorate ritual structures and sometimes simply served as ornately annotated (in Sanskrit) Balinese calendars called *tika*. These

*Traditional **Kamasan**-style paintings are still regularly created on Bali for both ritual and commercial purposes. The overview panel (left) and detail (above) are good examples of this first form of Balinese painting. These two examples are reproduced by courtesy of the Neka Museum, located just above Campuan-Ubud.*

paintings and time references featured puppet-like figures drawn in three-quarter view so that both eyes of a mythical character or creature were visible. They were usually painted on crude cloth, using natural ochres, blues, rusts, blacks, greens and yellows made of deer horn, animal bone, oil-lamp soot, leaf juices, clays and stones, or any other natural materials that could be made into paint. Upon completion the paintings were smoothed over with a seashell and then fixed with a diluted tree sap called *ancur*. It was a tedious, time-consuming process, and the final effect was that of an early, serialized cartoon strip, a precursor of sorts to what the Western world would later publish as comic books or the *Doonesbury*-style cartoon panels that appear in your daily newspaper.

Such Kamasan paintings achieved courtly respectability in the 17th century when one of Kamasan's celebrated artists, later known by the title "Sangging Mahudara," was commissioned by the Rajah of Klungkung to paint a special picture for his *puri*, or palace. That artwork attracted the envious attention of other notables throughout Bali, and for the next three centuries the Kamasan art style spread throughout the island and served as the standard form for flat art painting found in Bali — both in the homes of common people and in the opulent *puris* of the ruling aristocracy. The same is true today, and excellent new and periodically restored examples of Kamasan-style paintings can be seen on the ceilings and walls of Klungkung's Kerta Gosa (Hall of Justice) and Bale Kambang (Floating Pavilion) or in art galleries and museums in Ubud and Denpasar.

As noted in the preceding chapter on Western artists, the greatest turnaround or changes in Balinese art began taking place in 1927, the year the German artist Spies settled on Bali and began imparting his knowledge of drawing and painting techniques to the then tradition-bound Balinese. Under the initial tutelage of Spies, then the Dutch artist Bonnet who settled in Campuan-Ubud in 1929, Balinese artisans were influenced in many creative ways.

Though Spies and Bonnet were of similar social bents, their artistic training and temperaments were quite different. Spies' work was that of an idealistic, Gauguin-like dreamer, while Bonnet was an exacting draftsman-technician, but together they exposed the Balinese to the best of two important schools of artistic thought, and the very adaptable Balinese soon went their own creative ways. Probably Spies' and Bonnet's most important contribution, however, was their founding — in January 1936, in cooperation with the aristocratic Ubud brothers Cokorde Gede Raka and Gede Agung Sukawati — of the Pita Maha Painters' Cooperative, a still-active artists' association whose aim was to promote, exhibit and market members' works and to establish quality control guidelines for the ongoing creation of such works. Under the Pita Maha's guidance, Balinese art entered a period of efflorescence, or renaissance, that is still blooming.

Formally expressed, art in Bali, whether of *wayang* or Western derivation and influence, is simply a graphic manifestation of ritual behavior that has long been encouraged by the Balinese community, their complex religion and the personal spiritual drive that such factors release in individuals and the collective community. Art on this island is not — as is so often the case in most urban communities — a special, creative domain occupied by a select cadre of individuals called artists (and art critics). Nor is it an acceptable symptom of mutant behavior, the manifestation of a misunderstood neurosis, or some mystical free-fire zone visited only by spiritually-inspired visionaries.

Indeed, anthropologists like to point out that the Balinese language does not even have a word to identify what Western dictionaries define as "art". The Canadian media philosopher Marshall McLuhan (1911–1980) used to point this out in his writing and speeches by quoting a Balinese man who explained to him that "he simply did everything the best he could," whether he was ploughing a field, bundling grain or carving a piece of wood.

International collectors and critics of so-called "art" have for many decades simply tossed Balinese art — whether it be in the form of sculpture, painting or music and dance — into a catch-all category called "folk art." But in recent years, these self- or media-ordained culture vultures have been swooping back down for a second look as they are beginning to recognize the technical, symbolic and spiritual strength of many Balinese creations. Most of what they are seeing is indeed being produced en masse for touristic and day-to-day ritual use, but in one village or another, where stars shine brightly, they are now finding many brilliant gems of "artistic" behavior.

I Gusti Nyoman Lempad, (see facing page) was the grand old master of Balinese "modern" art. During his long life (he was said to be 116 at the time of his death in 1978), Lempad distinguished himself as a mask carver, architect and draftsman. "I feel I was reincarnated on this Earth to create what the Gods direct," he said before his death.

I GUSTI NYOMAN LEMPAD *(1862–1978)*
Durma bertemu dengan ibunya (seorang Bidadari),
Durma Meets His Mother (Nymph),
China ink on paper, (H×W: 40×25 cm), 1961
From the Neka Museum Collection

I GUSTI PUTU SANA *(1950–   )*
Dancing Frog, China ink and acrylic on canvas
(H×W: 62×84 cm), 1973
From the collection of Leonard Lueras

I DEWA PUTU MOKOH *(1935–   )*
Untitled, *acrylic on canvas*
(H×W: 140×190 cm), 1984
From the collection of Brent Hesselyn

IDA BAGUS MADÉ TOGOG (*1920–   *)
Ardjuna Wiwaha, acrylic on canvas
(H×W: 91×152 cm), 1966
From the collection of Wija Waworuntu

IN BATUAN
The World in Miniature

JUSTIFIABLY, THROUGHOUT RECENT HISTORY, the neighboring villages of Batuan and Sukawati, which comprise a specific administrative district in the south-central state of Gianyar, have been renowned for the prowess of their storytellers. Sukawati has long been famous for its *dalang*, or shadow puppet masters, and Batuan is a sprawling roadside village where *gambuh*, Bali's most classical form of dance-drama, and *topeng*, the traditional masked dance, have achieved state-of-

the-art recognition from both Balinese and visiting scholars. Batuan is also accordingly famed for the skill of its painters, who throughout the island are known for the attention they pay to minute symbolic and documentary artistic details. Fantasy artists such as Hiëronymus Bosch, W.C. Escher and Aubrey Beardsley would have felt at home in the art fields of the Ubud-Pengosekan area, but it is to Batuan that Indian, Persian and medieval Christian miniaturists would find kindred spirits and artworks. In a

recent essay about Balinese art, Dr. A.A.M. Djelantik, a respected local prince, physician and art authority, reported that Bali's Batuan-area artists have long been celebrated for their "miniatures, small paintings on paper exquisite in refinement, giving variations from the delightful to the mysterious and the demonic."

"More recently," Djelantik writes, "artists from Batuan perceived the encounter with modernization in a typically Balinese way — as a humorous theater performance, expressed in various comic paintings showing motorcars, helicopters and tourists with gigantic cameras and surfing boards in the midst of traditional Balinese village life."

Indeed, if small is beautiful and fun, perhaps no one artist from that talented village communicates this spirit with more humor and zeal than does I Madé Budi, an animated father of six girls and four boys whose finely detailed and whimsical works have been shown here and abroad to critical acclaim. Budi, who was born in Batuan's Banjar Pekandelan in 1932, is typical of many peasant class Balinese who by dint of birth as Balinese have grown up in a highly-charged creative atmosphere. Over the years he has achieved recognition by his peers as a dancer, flautist, woodcarver,

village elder and, of course, as a painter. All of these skills he learned either within the walls of his home (which was also his father's and grandfather's home), in neighboring compounds a few palm trees away, or during early evening jam sessions with other musicians, sculptors and painters. Budi of Batuan recalled during a recent interview that he started out "professionally" in the arts as a woodcarver. From the age of 10 to 13 he mastered this tedious task (carving picture frames most of the time), but he found that the part of carving work which he liked most was the drawing of preliminary carving lines on blank strips or blocks of wood. Told by others that he had a skill for drawing, he began taking instructions from other Batuan artists such as Ida Bagus Wija, Ida Bagus Togog and Dewa Kompiang. This was a painstaking apprenticeship in which one first had to execute fine pencil sketches on paper, then trace the pencil sketch carefully in permanent ink, and then, with a repetitious application of Chinese ink washes, assign the outlined figures varying degrees of opaqueness and translucency. After the desired lighting effects were achieved by such ink-layering, final oil, acrylic or watercolors were applied, and — in a final touching-up step — white or yellow highlights were dabbed here and there to bring the painting into a more finished focus.

Budi remembers with a laugh that he sold his first painting in 1946 for 7½ rupiahs "to a Dutchman who came to my house. I thought the painting was ugly-traditional," he says, but that sale encouraged him to pursue painting and shortly thereafter he began showing (and selling) his paintings in a downtown Denpasar bookshop. On the following pages is a small sample of some of his recent works.

Budi of Batuan stirs up some paint before continuing to work on the large life-size canvas behind him. Budi's Batuan style successfully combines and juxtaposes ancient wayang religious themes with 1930s artistic influences and contemporary reality, whether they be in the form of demons, a roving photographer or Australian surfers riding rococo-like beachbreak waves off Kuta Beach.

I MADÉ BUDI *(1932–)*
Surfing and Sakenan Island, *China ink*
and watercolor on paper (H×W: 48×68 cm), 1985
From the collection of R. Ian Lloyd

The following four paintings in this portfolio of artworks are by Budi.
They are from the artist's personal collection unless otherwise cited.

Windsurfing, Bali, *China ink and*
watercolor on paper, (H×W: 41×26 cm), 1985

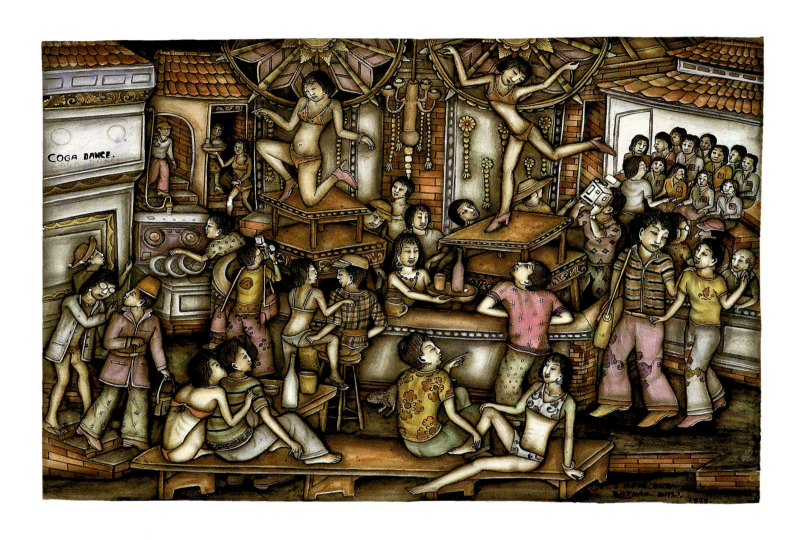

The Mississippi Queen Bar, Bangkok,
China ink and watercolor on paper,
(H×W: 24×36 cm), 1979
From the collection of Dean Barrett

The Desert Inn Casino, Las Vegas,
China ink and watercolor on paper,
(H×W: 32×32 cm), 1979
From the collection of Leonard Lueras

124

The 1906 Badung Puputan,
China ink and acrylic on canvas,
(H×W: 120×200 cm), 1981

MUSIC
In a Land of a Thousand Dances

TIME ON BALI IS A FLUID CONCEPT. LIKE ICE ON a sand dune, it simply melts away. Stay here for a while and you'll soon understand why. The pace is slow, sometimes even languid, but the days are incredibly full. Weeks are like days, months become weeks, and suddenly it's time to lift yourself from that comfortable tropical chair and leave. It's like a daydream in which you have been part of an epical series of events, but then — pow! — you wake with a start, look at your clock, and

realize you've only been asleep for a few minutes. Yes, time flies, but slowly, as if in a blossoming time-lapse film sequence photographed in slow motion.

The Balinese are, like tropical folks everywhere, easygoing, laid-back sorts. But when it comes to time notation, marking time, or what we in the West call "music" — well, that's another matter altogether. When an occasion requires music, the average Balinese musician (which means nearly everyone on the island) literally explodes into a blast of clanging, syncopated rhythms and aural time zones that are the envy of musicians throughout the world.

No one who has visited Bali and heard a particularly good *gamelan* ensemble will ever forget the curious, even spine-tingling rush of excitement that such an experience generates. Miguel Covarrubias recalls in his book *Island of Bali* that on his first night in Bali in the 1930s, he and his wife, Rose, were invited by the management of their hotel to attend a Balinese music concert being held in the hotel's gardens. The Covarrubiases showed up for the performance, but they were sceptical.

"We had experienced disappointments on such occasions elsewhere and we were fully prepared to hear another of the denatured versions of native entertainment usually concocted for tourists," he wrote. What they heard was another matter. Or as Covarrubias vividly recalled later: "It was an Oriental ultra-modern Bach fugue, an astounding combination of bells, machinery, and thunder. All of the pieces they played that evening were masterpieces of musical structure, simple, but rich and alive, violent and at the same time refined … ."

Another of Covarrubias' Thirties colleagues, the eminent American composer Colin McPhee, remembers that the first time he took music lessons from a

pair of *gangsa* players in the village of Kedaton, he began to hear what the Balinese call "flower patterns" or "voices" — "two different rhythms, positive and negative, that fitted together like parts of a puzzle to form an unbroken and incredibly swift arabesque. Each part raced along in nervous electric energy. It was a fugitive duet in Morse code … that broke the music into spangles, gave it light and fire, [and] created tension so that the longest phrase could not die."

McPhee, who spent some nine years in Bali, and later even composed a major Balinese-Western symphony, *Tabuh-Tabuhan* (which premiered in Mexico City in 1936 to critical acclaim), likened Balinese music to "a shining rain of silver" that "rose at one moment to a fury, and fell the next to an inaudible throb." At times, he wrote, it "unrolled like some ancient chant, grave and metallic," but on other occasions it was "blithe, transparent, rejoicing the soul with its eager rhythms and lovely sound … ." McPhee in a word, was musically *moved*.

Andy Toth, an American musicologist and longtime Bali resident who catalogued the late McPhee's papers and photographs about Bali while he was studying at UCLA, agrees with those glittering McPhee descriptions.

"His enthusiasm is understandable," says Toth, "because any musician who comes here finds Balinese music amazing." Toth, a self-described "gamelan groupie," is partial to Balinese music — his UCLA doctoral dissertation was titled "Tuning Models in Balinese Instrumental Music" — but for good reason. He is into bronze and percussion, and, as he explains with authority, "Balinese gamelan music is simply the ultimate in large ensemble music a la percussion being played anywhere in the world today. When it comes to interlocking parts, abrupt accelerations, sudden stops,

A human mandala (left) lays back during a performance of the popular kecak dance. This stylized dance, said to have been co-choreographed by the artist Walter Spies and the dancer-ethnologist Katharane Edson Mershon in the 1930s, is a modern derivation of an ancient sanghyang trance dance. More subtle, but equally as spectacular, is the whirling, swirling legong dance (above).

and multi-layered, synchronized instrumental parts, nobody can begin to match the Balinese. Their dove-tailed hold," he swoons in musical parlance, "is seemingly seamless."

What really astounds Western musicians, Toth notes, is that the Balinese perform all of their terribly complex musical movements completely by ear, without a conductor or score, and in time sequences that can include 5, 7 or even 17 beats to the bar. Some complex *gamelan* compositions, such as those performed to accompany the a capella *kecak* dance, sometimes have as many as 15 different parts layered together.

"The primary beat cycle is marked by the *gamelan's* large gong, but somehow," says Toth, "these guys maintain a nearly impossible beat framework out of which issues a single, pure and sweet orchestral sound. That's the wonder of Balinese music. And the real wonder of it is that they seem to do it so effort-lessly. They make it look and sound easy, but in fact it's terribly difficult to do as a group. "I hate to say this," he adds in summation, "but the music is like the rest of this culture — sometimes hard to believe."

Most people, especially musicians, would agree. But not everybody. One visiting journalist said recently that Balinese *gamelan* music "gives me headaches and makes my teeth hurt." And even Charlie Chaplin, that lovable Tramp of the silent films era, recalled in his official autobiography that when he first visited Bali in the 1930s and heard the ringing sounds of *gamelan* music for the first time he didn't really care for it. "I found their music cold, ruthless and slightly disturbing; even the deep doleful passages had the sinister yearn-ing of a hungry Minotaur," he wrote.

Indeed, though Balinese *gamelan* music might not be everybody's cup of rice wine, whether you like it or not you will be astounded by its proliferation on so small an island. The last time any kind of *gamelan* census was conducted, it was determined that there were at least 4,000 active bronze *gamelans* of one type only — the full ensemble *gong kebyar*. In addition, it was estimated that another 19 working types of metal *gamelans* were active, bringing the known total of *gamelans* on the island to more than 10,000. This survey only considered bronze *gamelans* and did not include "other" *gamelan* categories such as those made of wood or bamboo.

What this means is that on this island of 2¾ million people, which is roughly about half the size of Jamaica or about the size of the sultanate of Brunei or the American state of Delaware, there are more than 10,000 full ensemble orchestras, and almost all of these can play a nearly complete repertoire of the island's many traditional, religious, operatic and "popular" musical compositions. Delaware by com-parison is probably fortunate to have at least one officially recognized symphony orchestra.

Where there is music, of course, there is dance; and on Bali, where nearly every child begins receiving some kind of informal music and dance instruction at the age of 6 or 8, the dance repertoire is seemingly endless. Bali is indeed, to quote the title of an old Wilson Pickett song, "A Land of a Thousand Dances."

As every musicologist or anthropologist who has ever visited Bali soon discovers, it is almost impossible to even attempt to categorize and name the innu-merable dances of Bali. McPhee, for example, says simply that there are three categories of dance one can observe — those rehearsed, those improvised and those that are "uncontrollably performed in trance." He then notes that "the catalog [of Balinese dances] is endless, and [even just] an analysis of the many tran-sitional variations from ritual to secular dance is a [major and complex] study in itself."

Indeed, within a range of 10 or 20 square kilometers nearly anywhere on the island, a casual visitor, not to mention an observant scholar, might in one month alone observe and log, like a birdwatcher, some 50 different kinds of dances being performed. And as is all too often the case here, each of these dances will vary in form and content from one village to the next.

At one temple *odalan* (an anniversary festival), a platoon of warriors wearing floral rams' heads will be seen performing a ritual *Baris*, or warriors dance, as a prelude to a fantastic dance clash between a leonine *Barong* and *Rangda* witch-goddess. And, because tonight is a full moon night, every other *banjar* (neighborhood council) will be mounting a series of *mendet* (offerings) and *topeng* (mask) dances in a special supplication to the gods. Other neighborhoods might feel that such simplistic dances are not enough to appease spirits on the prowl on this night, so they will carry things further with a staging of a *Gambuh* (classical operatic drama), *legong* (Dance of the Hea-venly Nymphs) or even a *kebyar*, (a flashy modern style

Five ironically masked dancers *from Bali's prestigious ASTI, the Academy of Indonesian Performing Arts, pose after a performance of a telek-sandaran dance which was premiered in Sanur in 1986. Telek and* sandaran *refer to characters who danced with mythical* jauk *dancers in a classical version of the* calonarang *exorcism dance based on the legend of Rangda, queen of the* leyaks.

dance that first appeared about 1915). Meanwhile, in a jungle clearing just east of Batubulan, all is solemn and earnest as two young virgins drift into the trance-induced bobbings and weavings of an ancient village purification ritual dance called the *sanghyang dedari*.

The mind boggles, but this Balinese beat goes on, and on, and on, into the dark hours that precede dawn and a new day filled with more of the same.

Simply put, Balinese dancing is a highly refined, stylized form of entertainment in which every movement has been thought out (except in the case of impulsive trance dances) in terms of religious rituals, storytelling or musical accompaniment. It is somewhat similar to courtly Javanese dancing, but has also been heavily influenced by Balinese naturalism and elements of ancient black and white magic. The more standardized dances, which are basically human forms of *wayang kulit* shadow puppet theater, are purely theatrical and usually relate fascinating segments of actual history, mythology or religious gospels taken from the *Ramayana* or *Mahabharata* epics of the Hindu religion. In these dances, the most common themes are those preferred by people everywhere on this planet — war and peace, love and hate, and, most often, the fight between good and evil. Whatever their predominant theme, or story line, however, these myriad Balinese dance forms are always beautiful.

Beryl de Zoete and Walter Spies, who co-authored the standard reference on this subject (*Dance and Drama in Bali*, 1938), contend that the Balinese are imbued with such a natural and graceful sense of movement that they seem to turn even a mundane task into a form of dance. "The Balinese," they write, "are plastically gifted to an extraordinary degree and their power of rendering movement, whether in stone or pencil or the evolutions of the dance is equally astonishing or rare.

"Wherever he may be, idle or at work … the Balinese is so perfectly in harmony with his surroundings and so graceful in his poise that we almost have the impression of a dance."

Appropriately, Balinese composers and choreographers have created — and are still creating — scores and dance movements to express what they feel about the cosmos, their religion or even the simple little truths they encounter in day-to-day life. As in most cultures, there is a set repertoire of classical dances that are performed almost by rote, but there is also a dynamism at work here that allows for constant adaptation, revision and creativity to suit the times.

All dance on Bali, however, is serious business, whether in the form of a *sanghyang* trance ritual, in which the spirit flies free from the body, or in a tiki-torched tourist setting, where the main purpose is to entertain for money. Even during comic dance interludes, when a performer might feign a fart or wriggle in a lewd manner, the dancer and his or her accompanying *gamelan* never seem to lose artistic concentration.

Cast members of Batuan's renowned gambuh *operatic troupe (left and above) enact scenes from a "Tebekjaran" (Stabbing of the Horse) operetta which is derived from court dances performed during Bali's opulent Majapahit era. In the sad scene above, the group's leader, I Madé Djimat, and a lower-ranking minister console a horse character (the jaran) who has just fallen to the ground in battle.*

One of the most unusual Barong-Rangda performances you can see
in Bali is held periodically at the desa Krambitan in the Tabanan area.
It is called a tektekan because during such performances the Barong
and Rangda (left and above) dance to calonarang accompaniment by
an orchestral ensemble which plays music on special bamboo slit
drums that are euphoniously called tektekan.

The anthropologist Margaret Mead (1901–1978), in an essay on *Children and Ritual in Bali*, reported that when it comes to music and dance on this island, there is not a gap — as in Western cultures — between so-called professionals and amateurs.

"There are virtually no amateurs in Bali, no folk dancing in which people do traditional things without responsibility to an artistic canon," she wrote. Mead observed that "There are enormous differences in skill and grace and beauty of performance, but prince and peasant, very gifted and slightly gifted, all do what they do seriously and become, in turn, critical spectators, laughing with untender laughter at the technical failures of others. Between the audience that gathers to watch the play and the players there is always the bond of professional interest."

McPhee agrees. Audiences in Bali, he writes, "are critical. People will leave their village and walk fifteen miles to see a famous dancer or cast of stars. Their interest quickly wanes at dull performances; uninteresting or imperfectly trained dancers and actors frequently find their audience melting away long before the play is over. The play is of far less importance than the performance, and actors are admired for their appearance, style, declamation or the florid ornamentation of 'flowers' in their singing. Dancers appeal through technical perfection, their personal charm, and above all their hair's-breadth synchronization of movement with the rhythmic syncopated music." Indeed, there is no room for faking it here.

In this day of bemos and motorcycles it is doubtful whether many Balinese will still walk 24 kilometers to see a fine dance performance (though they may well drive 150 kilometers), but what Mead and McPhee said in the 1930s about professionalism still rings true. It is just such "professional" peer pressure, in concert with very real material and spiritual obligations, that keeps Balinese culture alive and well in an increasingly commercial and distracting world.

As in the case of straight music, Balinese dance styles are also learned by rote. Indeed, during the early stages of dance instruction, a child's body is literally molded into proper dance postures by his or her instructor. During this process, the teacher hovers over her charges and forcibly bends, pushes and shapes a young child's arms, legs, waist, hips, neck and head into correct dance positions. It is not uncommon to see a dance instructor take out a large ruler and whack a student sternly on the arm or buttocks when his or her instructions are being ignored. Eventually, new students get into the swing of things and began soaring through the stylized movements of a butterfly, nymph, warrior, weaver or other such traditional and modern dance interpretations.

Compared to Western dance, the movements of Balinese dance are more grounded and centered. There are no ballet-like leaps, spectacular kicks or furious running around on stage. Rather, the dancer

These three long-haired maidens (above), students from Bali's ASTI performing arts academy, take a break after performing their roles as sisiya *(disciples of Rangda) in a* calonarang *dance story. According to legend, such* sisiya *could turn themselves into* leyaks, *or witch goddesses, and dupe unsuspecting passersby.*

flows with gravity, reserving his or her most expressive motions to movements of the arms, wrists, hands, neck, head, face and — in mysteriously exotic counterpoint — the eyes. Body weight is delicately shifted from foot to foot in gliding and shuffling steps which are complemented by the exotic swaying and shimmying of the hips and shoulders. From a central starting point the dancer arcs, glides and zigzags across the stage in smooth forward or circular movements. As one observer described this process, the body is "transformed into a hieroglyph, a succession of hieroglyphs, of attitudes modulating from significance to significance like a poem or a piece of music."

McPhee floridly describes some of these complex dance mannerisms. "The hands," he writes, "are the 'flowers' of the dance. In simple ritual dance or intricate, studied performance they embellish all movement. In rhythmic passages they move alertly to the syncopated accents, or vibrate rapidly from the wrist with nervous, brilliant effect." He likens certain stylized hand movements to mudras, or "symbolic ritual gestures of the priest."

Eyes are yet another dance element. "Facial expression," says McPhee, "remains set in one of the basic representations of serenity or physical energy. In dramatic moments narrow eyes grow still narrower, round ones more staring. Eyes are slewed first to right and then to left to stress certain rhythmic accents."

Other Balinese dance movements include "the rapid shoulder quiver" (*engejen pala*) and a "slight rhythmic shifting of the head from side to side with neck erect" (*engotan*). Seen in live performance, all of these movements seem effortless, but as McPhee notes, Balinese dance technique "calls for complete muscular control in all parts of the body and an incredible degree of physical endurance."

As in all Balinese theatrical or ritual forms, each dance style is once again performed only to one particular kind of music, which, in turn, is usually provided by only one specific type of orchestra. That's why in Bali it is necessary to have so many different kinds of orchestral ensembles. According to tradition and religious strictures, only the right orchestral accompaniment will do if higher spirits are to be pleased by a dance or music presentation. A different kind of group, for example, will accompany a *wayang kulit* than will accompany a *legong*. Consequently even esoteric orchestral forms continue to proliferate on the island. In toto, these myriad forms of music and dance add up to a remarkable cultural legacy.

In comparing Balinese dance to that which has been traditionally performed in neighboring Java, McPhee writes: "While Javanese dance retains much of the two-dimensional character of the bas-relief or shadow play, the Balinese dancer emerges boldly onto the stage, becomes dramatically plastic, with three-dimensional movement which must be interesting from all sides, for his audience surrounds him."

Balinese children get into the swaying mood of religious ritual from as early an age as possible. In this particular circumstance, five young girls (above) perform a backyard pendet, or offerings dance, during a family temple ceremony held in the village of Batuan.

Visitors to Bali are often astounded by the dexterity exhibited by even tiny children during highly refined dance performances. This particularly arresting moment was captured during a gopala (cowherd) dance performance by 12-year-old Wayan Lotring of the south-central village of Batuan. Following pages: The "Semar Pegulingan" (Gamelan of the Love God) from the village of Batuan in nearly full ensemble. For an identification of each instrument being used, please refer to the book's Appendices section regarding Balinese music.

The Balinese is part of an inherited
order governed by a complicated system of laws, which are natural to him
because they are innate in the con-
science of his community. Within
this pattern he seems to find perfect
satisfaction. And just as the energy
of the village finds harmonious expression in the order of the village
law, so the energy of the individual
passes through the sieve of his body in
perfect distribution.

> — *Beryl de Zoete and Walter*
> *Spies, from* Dance and Dra-
> ma in Bali, *1938*

The Balinese child is exposed from
infancy to a gesture, posture system, to
a way of walking and a type of attitude
which makes him early susceptible to
the more formal patterns of movement
and sound which are characteristic of
his culture. The style of the Balinese
arts is imbedded deep in the form of
the simplest acts of everyday living.
From the point of early determinative
experience, everyone born a Balinese
may be said to have a high aesthetic
capacity, both as potential performer
and as critical spectator.

> — *Margaret Mead, writing ab-*
> *out* Traditional Balinese Cul-
> ture, *1970*

RELIGION
Communicating With the Unknown

FOLLOWING SEVERAL ISOLATED CENTURIES during which the aboriginal people of Bali had developed a system of spiritual beliefs based primarily on animism and ancestor worship, the island was, like many places in Asia, mentally turned around by the introduction of Buddhism and Hinduism. Prior to the introduction of those foreign ways, Balinese spiritualism had centered its religious energy on the veneration of nature, and — in later, more formalized periods — on ances-

tral megaliths and other genealogical abstractions that were often placed on or near stone platforms, or primitive, pyramidal *maraes*, of lava rock construction. These *maraes* are not too unlike those one sees on islands throughout Melanesia, Micronesia and also in Polynesia from Tahiti to Hawaii.

It was at these *marae* sites that Bali's original people gathered and ritually invoked the blessings of the sun, mountains, the sea and other natural phenomena. Still visible near *maraes* that are extant in old *Bali Aga* areas are male and female megaliths (the former upright, the latter prostrate) and meeting pavilions where crude stone seats, ritual backrests called *menhirs*, were long ago erected in orderly caste lines along the perimeter of these *marae* platforms.

In these ancient sanctified places the early Balinese conducted religious services and held community meetings. At propitious times they prayed to their particular vision of a god, or gods, and sought the counsel of ancestral spirits that occupy the high places, or volcanic mountains, that play such an important part in the scheme of things Balinese. Balinese religionists never seem to allude specifically to a form of volcano worship by the Balinese (they speak only of the spiritual "high places" or "revered mountain peaks"), but even in recent times the Balinese have shown a marked propensity for paying special homage to the creative — and sometimes destructive — forces that periodically rack their island.

Indeed, when a volcano has ceased erupting and all is calm again, large lava projectiles that have been ejected by the volcano are very soon designated as sacred shrines-objects and are paid homage to with regular offerings. It is also not coincidental that everything in daily Balinese life is oriented toward the

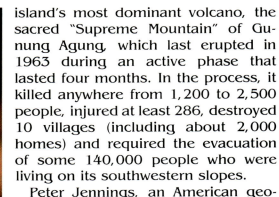

island's most dominant volcano, the sacred "Supreme Mountain" of Gunung Agung, which last erupted in 1963 during an active phase that lasted four months. In the process, it killed anywhere from 1,200 to 2,500 people, injured at least 286, destroyed 10 villages (including about 2,000 homes) and required the evacuation of some 140,000 people who were living on its southwestern slopes.

Peter Jennings, an American geographer who wrote a detailed master's thesis about this eruption for the University of Hawaii in 1969, reported that, "As thick layers of ashes and sand fell (from the skies around Gunung Agung), large agricultural areas (previously producing a volume of 316,518 tons of agricultural products) were buried and destroyed. As a result some 225,000 people were left without a means of livelihood. The *lahars* (hot mudflows) added further to the calamity. They destroyed entire villages (including Subagan and a part of the city of Karangasem) as well as roads, bridges and rice fields [and] killed over 200 persons." Jennings says that "the loss and damage caused by the eruption was estimated at 5,000,000,000 rupiahs (or in the value of the then current exchange rates, about 50 million US dollars."

Jennings doesn't directly pose the question of whether or not the Balinese are volcano worshipers, like the Hawaiians, but he is intrigued by the fact that Gunung Agung is revered by the Balinese as the "Navel of the Universe;" that Pura Besakih, the temple complex high on Gunung Agung's southwestern slope is considered to be Bali's most sacred and "mother" temple; and that one of the most sacred places in every other temple on the island (of which there are tens of thousands) is a shrine dedicated solely to that same mountain, Gunung Agung. He also points out that the

Hundreds of pilgrims bearing offerings throng the surf-pounded rock upon which sits Pura Tanah Lot (left), one of Bali's most sacred ancestral temples. This temple on the western Tabanan coast is one of Bali's six holy "national" temples. Above: A devotee clasps a kwangsen offering made of coconut leaves and flowers during a village temple's odalan (anniversary) celebration.

largest and most sacred ceremony in Bali, the rite of *Eka Dasa Rudra*, which is held only once every 120 years to purify the universe, is held at the Pura Besakih complex and is punctuated by the tossing of numerous animal offerings (everything from mice to eagles and bulls and horses, some 85 or more creatures in all) directly into the crater of Gunung Agung.

This rare *Eka Dasa Rudra* ceremony was actually being celebrated in March of 1963 when Gunung Agung suddenly erupted for no apparent or predictable reason and for the first time in living man's memory. The coincidence of this eruption during what was supposed to be such an auspicious time and occasion completely freaked out the Balinese, who saw it as an evil omen and proof that their highest gods were not pleased. Indeed, according to old *lontar* records the mountain had not erupted in any way since at least 1684 and, according to other scriptures, since the year 196 A.D. As a result of this untimely display of their gods' temperament, the Balinese called the entire *Eka Dasa Rudra* observance off and, following serious meetings between the island's most powerful *padandas* (or high priests), it was rescheduled for 1979, or the year 1900 according to Bali's own *Saka* calendar. This time the affair proceeded smoothly, without a heavenly hitch, and was widely photographed and written about by representatives of the world media.

Jennings writes in an epilogue to his thesis about Gunung Agung that since the 1963 eruption scientists have conducted extensive ecological studies and tried their best to educate the Balinese about how and why such things as volcanic eruptions happen (and how to avoid being affected by them), but he concludes that even with such data in mind "all may be proven invalid by such immeasurable and unforeseen factors as the belief in a god which could possibly nullify all systems of Western logic and rationality."

Logic and rationality? Perhaps it was due to a metaphysical search for such comprehensible explanations that the Balinese have during the past thousand years or so often looked outward and sometimes embraced other religions — or relevant aspects of other religions — to explain their fragile existence.

Probably the first waves of outside religious influence (i.e., Buddhism and Hinduism) landed on Bali's shores in the guise of early east Indian and Chinese traders who put in at this pleasant island to explore commercial possibilities and to stock up on the island's renowned pure water and plentiful foodstuffs. As noted in an earlier chapter, these traders were probably a mixed group that included wandering Chinese of Yunnanese descent and adventurous, seafaring Indians. The island of Bali was way out of the route for such travelers, but it was a natural land hop on the way to the famed Spice Islands to the east, so it is quite likely that these explorers stumbled onto its shores. It is generally known that these seafarers based in India were aggressively mounting commercial voyages to all parts of Asia, including the Indonesian archipelago, as early as the 1st Century A.D.. The big religious question, though, is who came first — a Hindu or a Buddhist?

A.J. Bernet Kempers, a Dutch archaeologist who authored the fascinating archaeological "guidebook" to Bali entitled *Monumental Bali* (1980), points out in a chapter on "Hindu Bali" that, "In Bali, as in all Indonesia, 'Hindu' is used in a more general sense than in India, where Hinduism and Hindu mainly refer to the Sivaist and Vishnuist religions and adherents. In 'Hindu-Javanese' or 'Hindu-Indonesian ...,' the 'Hindu' element refers to any influence or inspiration generally derived from India. In the domain of religion it also includes Buddhism. In this general sense 'Indic' (i.e. India-originated, widely spread over the surrounding countries, and variously integrated) might be a better word. We should not avoid it. In Bali 'Hinduism' and 'Hindu Bali' (Hinduistic Bali) refer to that complex phenomenon [called] 'Balinese religion,' and an entire way of life. It has a Sivaitic as well as a Buddhist aspect, but there are reminiscences of earlier Indonesian ideas and usages as well."

What Kempers is trying to say is that the Balinese religion, sometimes called "Balinism" to make things easier, is a mish-mash of various influences, depending on the culture's social, political or spiritual needs at a particular point in history. Or, as he tries to explain, "During their lifetime as a people the Balinese engaged everything with which they came into contact. They carefully chose what they wanted, rejected what they eventually did not like after having tried it out, thus creating a civilization of their own. They apparently did this repeatedly."

Consequently, what you see in Bali today may look like Hinduism, or even feel like Hinduism, but, on

During special festivals and big temple anniversary celebrations, Balinese women gather to prepare spectacular sarad offerings such as this one. These offerings, made of carefully sculpted and dyed rice dough, symbolize the Balinese universe. The central figure in this sarad found at Ubud is a Bhoma, which in mythology watches over the very vulnerable Middle World of humans.

closer examination, only cosmetically resembles what an Indian in New Delhi would puristically interpret as Hinduism. How do you explain that hairy, lion-like *barong* with chattering teeth that is so reminiscent of the many lion-dance creatures you've seen prancing around Chinese temples in Singapore? Or those eerie black magic nights, when the Balinese hide in their homes to avoid making contact with mysterious creatures called *leyaks* said to be lurking in the dark? Or rituals such as a tooth-filing ceremony, during which humans are transformed, Jekyll-and-Hyde-like, from temporal demons into human beauties?

All are part of the uniquely Balinese religious phenomena that drive visiting anthropologists and theologians batty. Such scholars find themselves disoriented, because Balinese religious and social beliefs are not just different from anything they have ever encountered anywhere else, but they differ on the island also — from province to province and even from village to village. As our man Covarrubias fondly, but frustratingly, disclaims in the introduction to his exhaustive book on Bali, "The details given here cannot be taken as applying to the entire island; each community has its own code, and what is law in one place is often ignored in the next. No two festivals are carried out in exactly the same manner and there are no two temples exactly alike. The general principles are the same everywhere, but the details vary from place to place and from caste to caste, and the tradi-

tions of the ancient mountain villages are different from those of the districts under the influence of the former rulers; to note them all would require an entire book for each custom or ceremony."

A story making the rounds of Kuta Beach's intellectual circles concerns the plight of a Belgian philosopher who for the past five years has been doing research on Bali regarding the Balinese definition of "truth." The poor man has spent many months on the island — interviewing people, compiling field notes, and comparing his observations with those made by other visiting scholars. After all that time, however, he has yet to write a single word on the subject.

Indeed, although Bali's religious guise is often readily identified by outsiders — and ritually and iconographically manifested locally — as a curious hybrid of Indian Hinduism, little has been written about the island's ancient links with India from an Indian point of view. One often wonders what Indians in India think about this quaintly "Hinduized" island east of predominantly Muslim Java. Is there a direct historical "connection" between India and Bali, or do folks back in Hindustan even care?

Recent studies indicate that such links do indeed exist. Proponents of this theory point in particular to the southeastern part of India that was known in olden times as the kingdom of Kalinga. It was from this area's coastal towns that those early Yunnanese and Indian seafarers set out on eastern bound trading

Candikuning, a lake spirits temple on the shores of Lake Bratan near Bedugul, honors the water goddess Dewi Danu. The stylized multi-roofed merus (or mountains) which rise above the temple compound are made of dark sugar-palm fiber. Such merus symbolize the Cosmic Mountain, Mahameru, home of Bali's (and Hinduism's) complex pantheon of spiritual and ancestral gods.

missions that eventually reached exotic places to the east such as Chittagong, Rangoon, Kra, Aceh and Kedah. After years of such trading and trial voyages, these intrepid travelers pushed even further south and east to Borneo, Sumatra, Java and, according to their oral histories, to a place of some historical and spiritual significance they called Bali.

Most of these early trading expeditions originated in the old port towns of Chandbali, Paradip, Cuttack and Chandipur, where descendants of the *kalingans* still speak an old Indian dialect called Orissa. It was from these Orissa-speaking people, scholars note, that other people of Southeast Asia first learned the now popular theater-cinema form called *wayang kulit*, or shadow puppetry. It was also from these eastern Indians that a specialized dye-before-weaving cloth-making technique called *ikat* originated. Both of these art forms are still popularly practiced there. Also particularly curious in this part of India, or Kalinga, are Bali- or Java- Prambanan-style temples that feature wide-mouthed *bomas* (stylized bears or *rakasa* demons) carved in stone over their entryway lintels.

Pending further study, this coincidental linking of traditional cultural practices in India to a small and distant island called Bali is perhaps a tenuous matter at best, but linguists like to note that the word *bali* in Orissan dialect means "sand." Conversely, the word "Bali," as interpreted by the Balinese, simply refers to their island, or, in the ancient Balinese *Kawi* dialect, to

someone that is very mighty, strong and able, or — in its noun form — to a hero. Perhaps this is a reference to the Hindu demon called "Bali," a dwarf *avatar* (*vamana-avatara*) who reigned over three mystical worlds coveted by Vishnu, the conservator and protector of worlds and restorer of *dharma* (moral order).

Whatever these ancient connections between India and Bali, the most fascinating and thought-provoking one is an annual commercial cum religious festival that takes place in the east Indian port town of Cuttack. In Cuttack, a coastal community about 450 kilometers southwest of Calcutta, the descendants of early Cuttack seafarers gather once a year to commemorate the departure many, many years ago of Orissan traders to a special and faraway place called Bali. During this yearly observance, called *Bali-jatra*, or the Bali festival, the people of Cuttack set small, lamp-like boats afloat in offshore waters and wish them, to the accompaniment of prayers, dancing and floral offerings, a safe and propitious voyage to Bali.

Indeed, even the Balinese people's preoccupation with the concept of a sacred mountain, or mountains, was borrowed in large part from Indian cosmology. In hinduized cultures throughout Asia, the idea of a Cosmic Mountain — usually identified as Mount Meru, Mahameru or Sumeru — is an important part of nearly all early Hindu-related creation epics.

In ancient Vedic manuscripts, Mahameru was the prime focal point, or spiritual axis, the "Father of All

Pura Besakih (above), which sits on the southwest slope of Bali's sacred Gunung Agung, is, according to author-scholar David Stuart Fox, "the unifying center of worship for all Hindu Balinese," and is often referred to as Bali's "Mother Temple." Within the village complex of Besakih are 18 public temples, 4 special "subsidiary" temples and numerous ancestral clan and family temples of all sizes.

This stream of pilgrims was photographed at Bangli during the annual Galungan festivities. During this great festival, the Balinese honor ancestral spirits who return to earth to dwell again in the homes and temples of their earthly descendants. During this time the Balinese put normal work habits on hold and celebrate for many days and nights.

A pemangku priest, Ida Bagus Rusna, offers special prayers within the Taman Pule temple at Mas on the day after Manis Kuningan. During Kuningan, which occurs ten days after Galungan, special offerings are made to appease the many positive and negative forces which hover about in the various spiritual and physical realms of the perpetual universe.

Humanity," on which the highest Hindu gods sat and ruled over the Universe. During the hinduization of Indonesia, this concept was brought closer to home by naming great peaks in a particular region after the legendary Mahameru. It is no mere coincidence, for example, that the highest peak on the island of Java, Mount Semeru (3680 m), was given that holy name. Following the conquest of Bali in 1343 by Hindu-Javanese rulers of the so-called Majapahit Era, this concept of a Mahameru holy mountain was transferred in name and spirit to Bali's Gunung Agung.

This regarding of the highest peak as a seat of the gods was readily adopted by the mountain-worshiping Balinese, and during the past six centuries — as the theologies of a mountain cult became formalized by Hindu precepts — the Cosmic Mountain theme greatly influenced nearly all religious and secular forms of expression on the island. The most obvious examples of such mountain motifs are in architectural structures such as the *candi bentar*, or split gates, that you see everywhere on the island. These entryways, which look like stepped towers that have been cut in half and separated into a gate, are said to represent two parts of the legendary Mahameru, one half being Gunung Agung and the other Bali's second most important peak, the active volcano Gunung Batur.

The other most prevalent mountain symbols on the island are the thousands of pagodas, or *merus*, which rise above courtyard walls like upside-down exclamation points and impressively punctuate nearly every holy place on the island with their stylized pyramidal roofs made of dark sugar palm fiber. These stylized "mountains" built on basalt stone bases always have anywhere from three to eleven roofs of receding sizes, the number of roofs being indicative of the Hindu deity or deities being honored. A tiered *meru* dedicated to Siva, for example, will feature eleven of these roofs, but those built in honor of Brahma and Wisnu have only nine. However many roofs are built, it is always an uneven number, in keeping with numerological beliefs and ancient rules of *adat* that maintain a sense of universal order on earth.

All of these *candi bentars*, *merus* and scores of other architectural and iconographic creations with similar motifs derived their inspiration from imported Hindu precepts, but like so many other things on the island, they are primarily, distinctively and uniquely Balinese.

Balinese ceremonial offerings are wrought in literally hundreds, if not thousands, of shapes and color schemes. Under umbrellas in the Pura Taman Pule at Mas (left) are an assortment of palm, flower and fruit offerings. While on this page (clockwise from top left) are a cili, a lamak, a tamiang on a car, and a tamiang on a roadside shrine.

LIFE CYCLES
Points of Universal Reference

MEDITATIVE CALM IS WHAT ONE WOULD usually expect during such a poignant circumstance, but in those final moments of spiritual liberation — when his soul began soaring with the smoke and rose through elemental wind into the heavens ... and when vendors below, in the earthly chaos of free enterprise, doubled their prices for cold beer, 7-Ups and clove *kretek* cigarettes... and when his much holy-watered and offerings-covered body had begun to crackle, flame and

shimmer like an opal beneath its black and gold sarcophagus — that's when the thousands of funeral faithful surrounding his pyre cheered louder, wishing His Majesty, the Agung, the High Prince and would-have-been King of Ubud, Bali, a rousing farewell.

"*Selamat jalan* — good journey," shouted a moved visitor from Java. And a British expatriate, who "knew the chap well," saluted the Agung's smoldering corpse with a glass of Bintang *bir*. "Here's to you, good Tjokorda," he toasted in a quiet voice.

Newly arrived foreigners murmured and gasped at the informality of this Brahmanic cremation spectacle, but "local foreigners," who have grown accustomed to such ancient sights in modern Bali, puffed on their *kreteks*, exchanged fond personal stories about the Agung's colorful life, and compared the happy scene unfolding before them to royal Balinese cremation rites they had observed 12, 25 and even 50 years ago in other Balinese kingdoms.

"Haven't seen anything quite so impressive since the last of the old Gianyar, Klungkung and Karangasem kings were burned," said an elderly Dutchman of Batavia and other colonial days past.

The next morning a reporter for Jakarta's large daily newspaper *Kompas* overestimated in print that some 250,000 people had squeezed into little Ubud town to bid the good Agung "adieu." And the home-island *Bali Post* later noted that, "In what was perhaps one of Ubud's most ostentatious displays of ceremonial ritual in this decade, the late king of Ubud, Tjokorda Gde Agung Sukawati, was given a final send-off last Wednesday, the 31st of January (1979)." In a six-page spread of cremation-day stories and photos the *Bali Post* guessed that 100,000 people attended the cremation and that an estimated 75 million rupiahs (at

that time about U.S. $120,000) — "and the energy of some 2,500 men and women ... not to mention many weeks of preparations" — were spent to stage this high caste cremation extravaganza. Both Indonesian newspapers questioned whether any Balinese royal family would ever again be able to afford, or indeed even be allowed, to produce such a costly and publicly extravagant last rite.

It is true that attendance at a cremation, or any of hundreds of cremations that take place on Bali every year, has become a somewhat commercial, morbid and crassly acceptable part of every tourist's weeklong itinerary in Bali; but this particular cremation — and all others, whatever one's birth caste — are important and extraordinary for a number of traditional and non-touristic reasons.

Most importantly, the Balinese believe fervently that the human body is merely a temporal shell for the soul's containment. When one's eternal soul leaves the body, death has occurred; but despite death, the soul remains in a sort of disorienting limbo and must be properly "purified, released and returned in proper, ceremonial style to that great Infinite Beyond."

In so-called *Bali Aga* (or "Ancient Bali") villages such as Trunyan in the mountainous Lake Batur area, the bodies of deceased persons are simply abandoned to the elements, Tibetan-style, to be decomposed and ravaged by the elements and wild animals. This is a now rare tradition that dates back to an animistic period in Bali's social evolution. These days, however, most Balinese dispose of their dead according to adapted Hindu rites that were introduced to their island by visiting holy men from India.

It is no longer *de rigeur* for widows of Balinese nobility to climb a tower, stab themselves in the neck

An array of rare religious objects (preceding pages) carry us into "Cycles," which are appropriately symbolized by the traditional ayunan roda ferris wheel (left) which is enjoyed by Balinese children during Galungan and Kuningan at a public site outside Klungkung. Above: A young devotee with a rice blessing on her forehead returns home after attending a home village temple festival.

When there is work to be done on Bali, everybody pitches in, regardless of their age or sex. These responsible and apparently happy children were photographed while helping out with a village construction project which was taking place above Ubud on the road to Sebatu.

or heart with krises, and then hurl themselves onto their lordship's pyre while releasing a white dove from their hands (in a customary act of *suttee*, as was common in Bali until late in the 19th century), but other traditional aspects of this final life-cycle rite endure much as they have been prescribed in ancient Sanskrit scriptures written in palm-leaf books, or *lontar*, by conscientious and religious ancestors.

The cremation of the Tjokorda Gde Agung Sukawati could have been conducted austerely, with little fanfare, but the Agung's people would have nothing of that. They were tradition-bound, whatever the cost or hassle, to accord him the respect and related royal prerogatives due a member of his ruling caste.

For one thing, the Tjokorda, who was 68 years old when he died on July 20, 1978 (of cancer of the liver), was modern Bali's most well-known prince. He was internationally renowned for his hospitality, patronage of Balinese arts, and for his unofficial role as a goodwill ambassador to worlds outside peaceful Bali. Kings, queens, heads-of-state and assorted jet-set celebrities often visited him, and sometimes sojourned for weeks at a time in private guest quarters he maintained within the spacious compound of his sculpted palace, or *puri*, in central Ubud. Among visitors who came to this quiet highland resort town and paid their respects at his *puri* were Queen Juliana of Holland, Queen Elizabeth and Prince Philip of Britain, Marshal Tito of Yugoslavia, several presidents of India, the King of Thailand, Sun Yat-Sen, Ho Chi Minh, then U.S. Vice-President Nelson Rockefeller, Robert F. Kennedy, Eleanor Roosevelt, the anthropologists Margaret Mead and Gregory Bateson, and the motion picture stars Charlie Chaplin and Marlon Brando. In 1974 Queen Juliana decorated the popular Tjokorda Agung and named him an officer in the Royal Dutch Order of Orange Nassau, citing his contributions to culture and international goodwill.

It is no wonder then that the people of Ubud worked feverishly for months to prepare a rich and traditionally complete cremation as a fitting climax to the Tjokorda's long and important life. His ritually prepared body was carried through the streets of Ubud atop a 21-meter high and 11-tiered *bade*, or cremation tower, and then spectacularly burned inside a huge black-and-gold bull sarcophagus. Alongside his Brahmanic bull was also burned a large red velvet and gold leaf Nagabanda dragon, a serpentine symbol of

Indeed, there are Balinese and there are Balinese. Wherever you go
on the island, you will be amazed at the diversity of character types
you will encounter along every road and byway. According to the most
recent census, approximately 2.75 million people now live on the
island, nearly all of them of ethnic Balinese descent.

royalty, that was empowered with a special "life" to carry the Agung's spirit to repose among his gods and royal ancestors. Fittingly, it was a proper medieval pageant at its Balinese best.

The Balinese rite of cremation is impressive indeed, but it is only one of the major life-cycle rituals which all living Balinese — and their survivors — observe on behalf of nearly every human born on this island.

The anthropologist Katharane Edson Mershon, in her fine field-study book *Seven Plus Seven, Mysterious Life Rituals in Bali* (1971, Vantage Press, New York), writes about what she called "the fourteen rituals in the stages of the Balinese life cycle." These rituals, as explained to her by a Balinese priest, involve "the first seven ceremonies a parent gives to his child," beginning with birth, and "the second seven, which the child gives to his parent" at the time of his or her death. It is a cycle that starts in amniotic fluid, "the water of birth, related to Wisnu, lord of waters," and ends when the body dies and is committed, first to Brahma, Lord of Fire, and later, back to the cleansing waters from which one entered — and now leaves — what we call life.

Long before a baby is born, a Balinese mother begins psyching herself up for the impending childbirth by carefully observing numerous spiritual and physical *adat* regulations regarding pregnancy and motherhood. Pre-natal customs vary from village to village and from family to family, but in nearly all cases they are strictly adhered to, because to be pregnant is to be "blessed" and close to a newly conceived emissary sent to earth by the gods.

During her field studies in Bali, Mershon carefully recorded conversations with various Balinese people who tried to explain to her some of these regulations. In a chapter she wrote on "Restrictions of Birth," a high priest identified as Padanda Madé pointed out some of the things a woman cannot do during pregnancy.

"A pregnant woman may not," Madé said, "eat anything containing fresh blood, such as *lawar* sauce which is composed of blood mixed with coconut milk. She is forbidden to eat water-buffalo flesh, roast pig, or octopus tentacles. That is the worst offence."

Octopus tentacles? The priest explained to Mershon that if a woman ate octupus tentacles during pregnancy, her afterbirth might cling to her, like an octopus, and "cause her great pain during delivery." Roast pig, on the other hand, might "turn her body bright red, causing heat." And blood is always bad because it is *sebel*, or unclean. It is for that same unclean reason that women are not allowed to enter a temple when they are menstruating. To do so would contaminate a holy place and tempt misfortune.

The priest's list of pre-natal restrictions continued: "She may not look at anyone who has a sore, or an open wound, or any discharge of blood. She may not gaze at a dead person, or attend any ritual pertaining to death. She may not eat food prepared by any person whose family is unclean, *sebel*." Consequently, given

the chance of such things happening, Mershon observed that Balinese women stayed at home as much as possible during pregnancy.

These various restrictions are numerous, but in addition to such don'ts an expectant mother also has to make regular purification offerings to the gods to ensure a safe and sound delivery of her baby. Such offerings vary in style and frequency depending on a woman's caste, religious fervor and the proscriptions of family or village priests.

Most pregnancy matters are attended to by the woman of a particular household, but once labor begins, it is considered proper for a woman's husband to be with her and assist her with the final birthing process. When possible, birth should take place in the woman's home, and her husband should remain near her, usually in a supportive position behind her, as she begins final labor pains and gives birth

The traditional manner of giving birth in Bali is in a squatting position. To achieve this position, and to take advantage of gravity during birth, the mother is usually propped up in a primitive birthing chair made of a large wooden plank raised above the ground. Behind her, serving as a back support, is her husband, who massages her abdomen, braces her with his legs, and comforts her during her ordeal. In front of her, to receive the new baby, kneels a doctor, priest or midwife, depending on local custom.

Once the baby has been born, the father should cut its umbilical cord with a bamboo knife (never a metal one) and stash the cord away in a container for future ritual use. Also, the birthing attendants should retain samples of amniotic fluid, blood and the entire afterbirth placenta. These matters are gathered together and placed into two coconut shell halves along with a *lontar* leaf that a priest has inscribed with magical religious symbols. The coconut shells are then tied together with sugar palm fiber and buried in the ground fronting the baby's new home.

Above this afterbirth burial plot is raised a bamboo support pole on top of which sits a small house-shaped shrine that has been built especially for this special occasion. These mini-shrines, called *sanggah tjutjuk*, are made of bamboo and usually are distinguished by little dark palm-fiber rooftops. Once they have been raised above the placenta's burial site, assorted baby-food offerings are placed inside them. These cute little *sanggah tjutjuk* shrines announce to all passersby that a baby has recently been born to the household. If the baby is a boy, the shrine appears at the right side of an entryway; and if it was a girl, at the left side.

The baby's umbilical cord, meanwhile, has been carefully wrapped in a container, and is usually kept in safekeeping below the mother's and child's bed mattress and bedboards until it has withered and dried. Later, the natal cord is put into a small gold or silver box and worn around the baby's neck as an amulet.

This is a very simplified recounting of the Balinese

Bali High? Showing their colors and being true to their respective schools are these two platoons of girls (left and above) who were captured in respective formations during a recent marching competition held in Denpasar. Such annual contests, which pit students from various junior and secondary schools against each other, are a popular part of modern Balinese campus life.

birthing process, but it demonstrates how much serious attention is paid to the initiation of a new human life. These birth rites, however, mark only the beginning of a lifetime of such life-cycle rituals. Indeed, during infancy alone, untold dozens of other customary procedures are also observed — regarding feeding, bathing, sleeping, walking, talking, and so on, ad infinitum. Proud and tradition-bound parents also ritually observe special offerings ceremonies on a baby's 3rd, 12th and 42nd days after birth, plus, for extra spiritual measure, the end of the baby's third month and first year. Depending on a family's caste, finances and parental pride, these various observances can be private, family affairs, or costly musical and theatrical extravaganzas that involve an entire community. Ideally, these ceremonies are held on auspicious days in the Balinese calendar.

At the time of a child's first year birthday, which is 210 days after birth according to the Balinese Saka calendar, he or she is dolled up in fine clothing and adorned, depending on a particular village's custom, with gold or silver bracelets, anklets and other jewelry. At this time, the baby's hair is also shaven nearly clean except for a long forelock of hair that is left growing on his or her forehead. This tassle of hair is retained so that the baby can continue to ward off illness.

Following the various rites of infanthood scheduled during a child's first year, most personal ceremonies are dispensed with until the time of coming of age, or adolescence. For girls, such observances correspond with the appearance of their first menses. "First blood" is a significant development in every Balinese girl's life, because it announces to the community-at-large that she is now a woman. The coming of age time for boys is a trickier matter, because such a time is difficult to determine. "Strangely," writes Mershon, "a boy's manhood often was judged by his sister's menses; for when that event occurred the boy would be deemed 'of age', particularly if they were at all close in age bracket."

"A boy comes of age gradually and unconsciously," writes Covarrubias, "but the first menstruation of a girl (*nyatja*) is an important event and when this condition arrives to the daughter of a prince, the village *kulkul* [signal drum] is beaten to announce that the little princess is now a woman of marriageable age."

Both Mershon and Covarrubias observed that in the case of young girls, once they have begun their first menstrual period, they are deemed *sebel*, so they are hidden away in a small hut until their periods end. Following this period of seclusion, a special purification ceremony is scheduled for an auspicious day. This public ceremony has strong sexual overtones, and includes special offerings and prayers in honor of deities of fertility and love. It is a joyous, humor-filled occasion, slightly naughty, but nice.

Another coming of age rite that usually coincides with puberty, but is sometimes postponed until after marriage or later, is the fascinating tooth-filing cere-

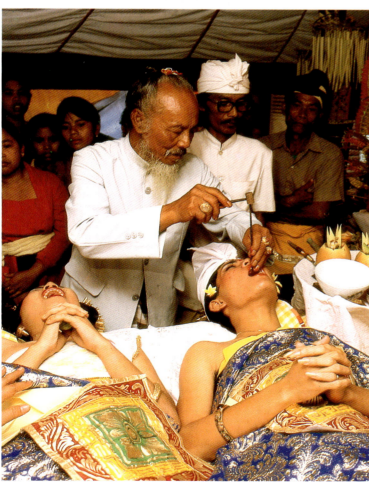

The children of Mr. and Mrs. Ida Bagus Sutarja of Mas gather in their
ceremonial best (left) before taking part in a ritual Balinese tooth-
filing (above). During the ceremony, a presiding priest (clockwise
from top left) blesses the offerings; "tattoos" a golden prayer on to a
woman's chest; then proceeds to file down the "demonic" fangs of his
young devotees. Tooth-filing is a mandatory life-cycle ritual.

mony which every Balinese person is obliged to undergo before his or her death. This extravagant and somewhat painful ritual, which dates to a more animistic period in Bali's social evolution, serves as an initiation into adulthood and humanhood.

The practical purpose of this primitive form of dentistry is to file down one's top and bottom front teeth until they are of a neatly uniform length. This is accomplished with a small metal file that is ceremoniously scraped back and forth across the teeth's protective enamel. Once this filing is completed, one's canines and incisors are worn down into a neat, piano-like line. This procedure seriously diminishes one's ability to rip and tear at meat products, but that is exactly what the Balinese have in mind. According to local custom, only "lower" animals and demons have fangs, so to distinguish "higher" humans from such rudimentary and inimical creatures, particularly in the judgement they will face in the afterlife, these animal-like teeth are cosmetically altered.

This transformation process only takes a few grating minutes, but because it is considered to be an important rite of passage, such tooth-filings are accompanied by much pomp and ceremony. At a typical tooth-filling ceremony, musicians and sometimes dancers and puppeteers are invited to perform, a great feast is laid out in the home for the immediate family, relatives and invited guests, elaborate offerings are constructed, and those whose teeth are being filed

are meticulously made up and costumed in fine brocades, silks and other ritual wear. It is a decidedly expensive visit to the dentist.

In olden times, this filing process was much cruder and painful, but in recent years the priests who preside at such rituals have been advised to limit their filing to the minimum strokes necessary to accomplish their symbolic job. One young man who was having his teeth filed a few days before he was due to leave Bali to begin studies at the University of California told a foreign observer that visiting dentists have greatly influenced and toned down this process. "Another reason the priests don't file the teeth so low anymore is ice cream," he said. "We know that if our teeth are filed down too much, we won't be able to eat ice cream."

After one's teeth have been filed, and one is deemed to be a properly beautiful human being, the next most important rite of passage before death and cremation is marriage. Earlier in this century, the most common form of marriage involved an actual kidnapping of a prospective bride, sometimes against her will. Today, however, marital procedures are more westernized and characterized by mutual consent between lovers and their families — except in the case of pre-arranged marriages, which are still somewhat common.

The idea of a husband kidnapping his wife is still perpetuated in some villages, however, by a quaint custom called *ngorod*. Kidnapping is probably too strong a term for this romantic procedure, because a

The occasion is the Pengerebongan, a Barong-Rangda trance ritual staged bi-annually at Kesiman, and this particular group of checkered priests and warriors are reenacting a battle scene that took place in the Kesiman area during ancient times. They first mendet *dance into the Kesiman temple's inner courtyard (above), then fly into a fitful,* kris-*wielding trance (right).*

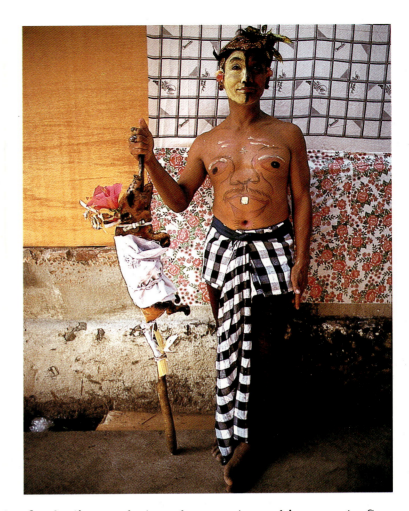

ngorod is actually what in the West would be called a good and old-fashioned elopement.

During a proper ngorod, two lovers make "secret" arrangements to meet and run away to a hiding place, usually the home of a friend in another neighborhood or village. The word secret is used, but it is usually an open secret that has received the tacit approval of friends and relatives. Once a daughter has been kidnapped, though, her family will feign surprise and outrage and even go looking for her. Such irate reactions are greeted, of course with sly chuckles. Eventually, the bride's family cools down, the lovers comes out of hiding, and everybody happily attends their pre-arranged wedding ceremony.

Once the various "living" cycles of human existence — birth, infancy, adolescence and adulthood — have been properly completed, only one last stage in life remains: death. Life, according to Balinese theology, is but a temporal, recurring blink of time in the ongoing evolution of the eternal soul, so the end of one's life is not regarded as a dreadful, grand finale; rather, so-called death marks a joyous and new beginning, or a time of spiritual rebirth.

Central to Balinese attitudes regarding death are hinduistic doctrines of transmigration, reincarnation and karma. According to such concepts, the souls of humans, the highest of God's earthly creatures, will continuously be reincarnated — and undergo periodic spiritual testing — until they prove themselves worthy of salvation and eternal peace (an achievement often referred to as being in a state of Nirvana, or oneness with God). Until this happens, one's indestructible soul will simply ricochet back and forth between temporal lives on earth — in one form or another, depending on one's karma, or previous life acts — and variable sojourns in either heaven or hell.

Therefore, if you have earnestly followed the right way toward ultimate purification, you may remain in Nirvana, or, if necessary, return to yet another cycle of life as a higher caste person who is one or more steps closer to godliness. If you have failed during your most recent testing period, however, you may be reborn into an even lower form and have to begin a long, tedious cycle of spiritual evolution all over again.

In keeping with positive thinking, every Balinese hopes to move on to a higher plane of existence, so at the time of death, his or her relatives cover all spiritual bets by giving the departed souls of their ancestors a last and great send-off to the heavens. The proper cremation and spiritual liberation of a loved one is a Balinese person's most important earthly duty, so no amount of energy or expense is spared to insure that his or her soul is properly prepared for reception into the afterlife. This is accomplished, in grand style, by purifying one with earth, fire and water.

In the Bhagavadgita, "The Lord's Song" published in ancient Vedic manuscripts, it is said that, "The end of birth is death. The end of death is birth. That is the law."

Preceding pages: At Bubunan, not far from Singaraja on Bali's north coast, the children of a recently deceased Bubunan resident await the beginning of the final cremation day ceremonies in honor of their ancestor. "Strange as it seems," writes the author Miguel Covarrubias, "it is in their cremation ceremonies that the Balinese have their greatest fun." Fun, yes, but in a serious, spiritual way.

On cremation days an unusual, festive tension pervades the air.
Shortly before the ritual rites begin, a village priest (far left) burns
incense and a painted devotee (near left) arrives on the scene with a
skewered babi guling (suckling pig). Balinese-style pallbearers
(above) whirl the cremation tower (badé) and corpse around in circles
so that the deceased's spirit will not later find its way back home.

By force of habit, the soul lingers near the body when death comes, and remains floating in space or lives in a tree near by until liberated by the obliteration of the corpse by the elements: by earth, by fire, and by water, to destroy the last unclean tie that binds the souls of the dead to this earth. By cremation the soul is released to fly to the heavens for judgement and returned to be reborn into the dead man's grandchildren. Failure to liberate the soul by neglecting to perform the cremation or by incomplete or improper rites would force the soul to turn into a ghost that would haunt the careless descendants.

> — *Miguel Covarrubias on "Death and Cremation" in* Island of Bali, 1937.

The burning body of Ubud's "king," the Tjokorda Gde Agung Sukawati, glows under the charred remains of a black and gold bull sarcophagus and a sinuous nagabanda dragon during his spectacular cremation ceremony held on January 31, 1979. Later, the Agung's ashes were scattered at sea in a final act of ritual purification of his soul. Photo by Leonard Lueras.

PATTERNS
From Day-to-Day and Year-to-Year

QUIET AND DARKNESS WAS ALL THAT EXISTED IN the Beginning. Then one day this black stillness was enlightened and illuminated by a vibration, a sound. This sound — AUM — signaled The Creation, and from that sound radiated a powerful light, or energy, in the inseparable, three-part form of Ang, *Dewa Brahma*, The Creator; Ung, *Dewa Wisnu*, The Preserver; and Mang, *Dewa Siwa*, The Destroyer. Together as one, Ang, Ung and Mung created the great sound — AUM — and in this

tripartite form were the great energy source we call "God." In turn, this trinity ruled over the three universal realms of the infinite cosmos — the high realm of gods (*Bur*), the middle realm of humans (*Bwah*), and the lower realm of demons (*Swah*).

This Balinese *Tri-Loka*, or three part division of the Universe, also marks, in a neo-Hinduistic way, the beginning of the many patterns, symbols and "right ways" that explain and regulate the existence of man, his gods and everything else on the island of Bali.

On Bali, nothing just happens. Rather, everything is logically and fatefully part of a cyclical and eminently explainable universal order that will remain harmonious and predictable as long as man works hard to keep it that way. Indeed, because evanescent man occupies the middle realm — between the white, righteous and positive gods and deified ancestors of the heights (the mountains) and the black, evil and negative demons, devils and other antagonistic spirits that live in the sea — he has to constantly and aggressively maintain a spiritual balance, or harmony, between those two constantly opposing forces.

To achieve a check on these metaphysical protagonists and antagonists, the Balinese have over the centuries created an elaborate system of religious symbols, rituals and day-to-day actions designed to strike a peaceful balance between all known and/or abstract opposite forces, whether they be good and evil, life and death, strength and weakness, health and sickness, or, even, man and woman. By way of explanation is this fascinating example:

Several years ago an American journalist, pleased by what he had seen in Bali, took a fine painter from the south-central village of Batuan on a tour of Asia and the West Coast of the United States. The artist, a mature man of 48 who had taken two wives and fathered seven children, had never left Bali, but he was excited by the prospect of seeing faraway places he had only read about in books and magazines. The artist was confident and inspired by the thought of travel and the new knowledge and experiences it would bring, but at the same time he was quietly terrified at the prospect of flying away in a big Garuda airplane for the first time in his life. He had several months to prepare for his journey, so during this time he sought the counsel of village elders and made regular "wish-me-good-luck" offerings at the big ancestral temple in a corner of his sprawling *desa* (village compound). Finally, when the big departure day arrived, he said goodbye to his family, village and Bali. And for the first time in anybody's memory, tears filled his eyes as he turned and looked at Batuan for one last time before leaving for Ngurah Rai Airport.

The first leg of his journey took him — in about an hour's flying time — to the central Javanese city of Yogyakarta. There, he was greeted upon arrival by an old friend who took him and the American journalist to his spacious home off busy Jalan Malioboro. Everything was comfortable and familiar here in Yogya — no sudden culture shocks to experience since he was still in Indonesia — but the first thing the Balinese artist did after being shown to his bedroom was curious indeed.

"*Permisi*, excuse me," he said to his host, "but I have to find out where I am." With those words he reached into a small, cloth shoulder bag and took out a green army compass he had packed away with other personal belongings. Compass in hand, he proceeded to pace the length of the room twice, turning now and then to

Geringsing cloth (left) is one of the artistic wonders of Bali. This rare form of double-ikat cloth, which is designed and dyed on tied threads before the warp and weft are woven together, is indigenous to the Bali Aga village of Tenganan, east Bali. In olden times, human blood was mixed in with the geringsing dyes. Above: A wayang detail from a sarong length of gold and silk songket cloth.

determine magnetic north. After fixing north, he marked his location on a pocket map and plotted out a straight line between Yogyakarta and Bali.

"*Aduh! Bagus*," he exclaimed happily. "Now I know where I am. And with that he began to rearrange the furniture in his bedroom so that his head would be facing toward Bali when he slept. He explained later that he had promised his family that he would always sleep, wherever he went, with his head pointed in the general direction of Bali's sacred Mount Agung.

As his long journey progressed, he repeated this little direction-finding and bed-moving ritual whenever it was practical. Sometimes, say in an elegantly appointed hotel room in Tokyo, this was an awkward procedure, so he would instead sleep upside down in the hotel bed, or move to a more mobile couch.

That Balinese artist's behavior was curious indeed, but what he was doing, wherever he slept, was adhering to ancient codes of conduct and traditional practices that are known throughout Indonesia as *adat*. To ignore such ritualized rules and patterns of behavior would tempt calamity, so to avoid possible misfortune during his journey abroad, he remained Balinese in spirit and actions.

Such *adat* regulations preoccupy the secular and ritual behavior of every Balinese from the time of his or her birth until death. In the case of the traveling artist, he was adhering to Balinese principles regarding spatial orientation and spiritual protocol. By constantly keeping himself in line with Bali (and the sacred mountain Gunung Agung), he was first of all avoiding a feeling of "getting lost," or what the Balinese call *paling*. The idea of being "lost" — or being out of touch with one's environment — terrifies the average Balinese, because if you are lost, you are out of sync with nature and susceptible to evil spirits, bad *karma* and other negative forces.

The American anthropologist Jane Belo has written in a 1970 article about Balinese temperament for the Columbia University Press that the Balinese are so acutely conscious of "their position in relation to the surrounding space of their world" that once their sense of direction has been turned around they "not only feel uncomfortable" but often are "unable to function."

"This theory is supported," Belo writes, "by the fact that the average Balinese, although he has plentiful supplies of distilled *arrack* and palm wine, does not

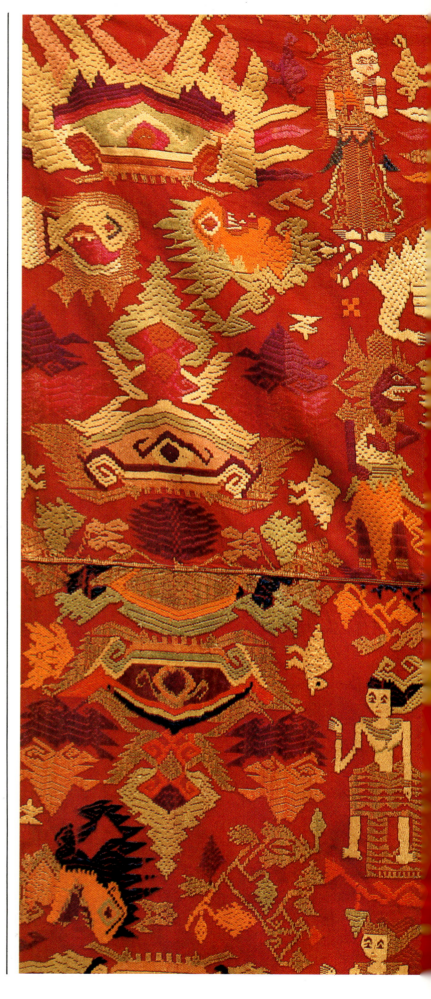

This fine piece of songket cloth features a number of classical wayang characters woven into its overall design. Added to the dyed silk material are decorative gold and silver weft threads which give the fabric a raised dimensionality quite different from other Balinese fabrics. This particular detail is from a cloth in the collection of Verra Darwiko of Denpasar.

like to get drunk. The feeling of confusion, the lack of his usual surefootedness and sense of equilibrium are so unpleasant to him that he does not often risk the experience. And the whirling of the universe which precedes nausea is positively terrifying. Then he is indeed *lost*." Belo recalls the example of an eight-year-old Balinese child she took to a distant village one day for dance instructions. During the course of a car ride to the unfamiliar village, the child lost his sense of direction, became *paling*, and refused to pay attention to his dance teacher. Once the child was returned home, he was fine, but when the same journey was repeated several days later, the boy once again went *paling*. "He grew anxious and was unable to eat and sleep. Then someone thought of taking him out into the fields, where he could see the high cone of the Gunung Agung, the highest mountain, rising to the north. He was cured of his trouble on the spot and had no recurrence of it during the six weeks of his stay in the village. He seemed happy there and made great progress with his dancing."

This matter of spatial orientation also applies to other aspects of Balinese behavior. Balinese, for example, dislike standing on their heads or doing somersaults for fear of becoming disoriented. And falling down, notes Belo, "is considered an unlucky sign, a presage that worse things may happen, occasioned by the evil forces which are only 'trying their strength' in causing the harmless fall . . . . Falling is a

shock which upsets the nice balance of well-being, just as the feeling of a rush of blood to the head in an inverted position is uncomfortable, and must therefore be wrong." The idea is to remain upright, or grounded.

Consequently, if a mischievous child climbs up a coconut tree and falls to the ground, he is not scolded because he was naughty, but rather because he exposed himself, and possibly his family, to inimical spirits. His parents will indeed be upset about the fall and the injuries suffered by the child, but they will be even more concerned about the unseen negative forces that caused the fall. To placate the disruptive spirits that caused the accident, special prayers and offerings will be made at the accident site by family members and, in many cases, a village priest or priestess. Another reason such rituals are observed has to do with Balinese beliefs that when one is suddenly jarred, say in an automobile accident or bad fall, a part of his spirit is forcibly knocked out of him or her and has to be ritually wooed back into the body so that all will once again be *harmonious* and *in balance*.

This positioning of oneself in relationship to the universe also manifests itself in customs having to do with good manners. Our Balinese artist, for example, slept with his head pointed toward Gunung Agung not just to establish his sense of location, but also because in Bali the feet are considered dirty and should never be pointed towards a holy place or person. For that same reason, one's sacred head should also never be pointed towards the ground because the earth we walk on is an "unclean" area frequented only by the body's lower realm, the feet. It is for this same reason that you will notice that nearly all Balinese infants are hand-carried everywhere and not allowed to touch the ground until they are old enough to stand up by themselves. This is not only because to allow them to crawl on the ground would be an unclean act, but also because to allow a child to do this would be allowing him or her to move about like an animal. Only lower creatures move around on all fours.

All of these *adat* considerations correspond, once again, to the Balinese people's preoccupation with space and structure. And once again, the Balinese use a religious metaphor, the Tri-Loka, to explain how this works. What the Balinese have done is apply the Tri-Loka breakdown of the universe to every other aspect of life as they know or have known it.

*"**The keris is far more** than simply a dagger to be used in war or an heirloom passed on from generation to generation out of reverence. The accumulated powers of one's ancestors slumber in the family keris. It is venerated like a family deity . . ." — from Urs Ramseyer's The Art and Culture of Bali. The above gold-and-jewel studded royal kris is from the fine antique collection of Verra Darwiko.*

This sacred pratima temple goddess sculpture from the offshore
Balinese island of Nusa Penida (above) has been known to induce
people into a state of trance. It and a matching male figure
(background) are carved from sandalwood, painted with gold leaf and
natural colors, and inset with rubies. They are about actual size here.
(H×W: 22×6½ cm). From the collection of Verra Darwiko.

This intricately-designed ceiling of wood and bamboo (above) is a modern Balinese interpretation of a traditional wantilan pavilion roof. Such roofs traditionally sheltered cockfighting arenas, but this one is being used to add ambience to a popular restaurant in the Kuta Beach resort town. Right: A tobacco-drying shed being built near Bangbang.

As noted in the introduction to this chapter, the Cosmos is made up of *Bur, Bwah* and *Swah*, or the high realm of gods, the middle realm of humans and the lower realm of demons. In the same manner, the island of Bali is divided into three parts — the sacred heights, the in-between area where people live, and the low, demon-filled sea. By extension, villages, homes and even the body are divided into three corresponding parts. The most sacred part of a village or living compound, for example, is always on the side nearest the mountain, and profane areas, such as a cemetery or a toilet area are always on the seaward side. Likewise too, a person's head, the seat of the spirit and the soul, is sacred; the body is the middle, life-sustaining repository of vital organs; and the feet are generally regarded to be unclean or impure. For this reason, you should never point or place your unclean foot towards or on anything sacred, including people; to do such a thing is to profane that which is "underfoot".

Two words that you will often hear in Bali that are related to these concepts of space, elevation and direction are *kaja* and *kelod*. To be oriented towards the mountain is *kaja*, or sacred, and to be oriented away from the mountains (toward the surrounding sea) is *kelod*, or the converse of that which is sacred. This doesn't necessarily mean that the sea is a bad place, but rather that it lies in opposition to that which the Balinese consider most sacred. It is a linear concept that explains in part how the Balinese have neatly organized their universe, island, villages, homes and even their sense of self. It also explains in a logical and even metaphysical way where and why things are built or ordered the way they are in Bali.

For all the above reasons, you will soon discover in Bali that such concepts are applied to even the most practical functions of everyday life. When rice is gathered and bundled, for example, it is always placed on the ground head up. Also, no Balinese carpenter would ever think of building a house with wooden pillars that are erected upside down. To do so would be to ruin the harmony or balance of a home, so one must always position a support beam with the timber's root end pointed toward the ground, not up and away from it. To do otherwise would be an impure act and would invite bad luck into a household.

A second line of conceptual thinking that will help a visitor understand Balinese reasoning and patterns of Balinese thought and behavior is a philosophical

approach to life that is summed up by the three words *Desa, Kala* and *Patra*. These words respectively mean Location, Time and Situation, and they are usually expressed together, in order, to explain why something has been done the way it has been done, even though it has been done differently from the way in which other people have done or would have done it. Keep these words in mind, because they may one day bail you out of a situation that defies rationale.

In practice, this three-part phrase, *Desa-Kala-Patra*, serves as a sort of convenient escape clause or catch-all answer to justify or explain aberrant, different or sometimes illogical ways of doing something. As one writer has explained, "there are about as many customs, habits, philosophies, traditions and viewpoints as there are Balinese," so points of view regarding behavior will differ from person to person and from place to place depending on what, where, why and how something has occurred. Each village also has its official *lontar* of *awig-awig* (regulations), which may differ greatly from those of the next village only a kilometer down the road.

Indeed, if you would like to frustrate a Balinese person who is particularly concerned or curious as to why you did the strange thing you just did in a particular situation, simply shake your head and say, "*Desa, Kala, Patra*." He or she will smile and understand immediately the situation ethics at work in your particular unexplainable circumstance.

Until the year 1954, the upper torsos of these buxom waterspouts at Goa Gajah were placed, curiously, on either side of the entrance to the Goa Gajah's famous "Elephant Cave." Then following archaeological excavations in the area, matching lower torsos were found alongside a former bathing site nearby. These ancient body parts were put together and the result is the creation of this spectacular, thousand-year-old Balinese bathing pool.

The Goa Gajah, situated on the road from Peliatan to Bedulu, can be easily found. The site is indicated by a concentration of curio shops. Today it is difficult to realize that until 1922 or '23, this well-advertised antiquity was known only to the local people. It is even more remarkable that it is a comparatively short time since an extensive watering-place was discovered [in 1954]. Its existence was not suspected even to the villagers.

> — A. J. Bernet Kempers, writing in his book Monumental Bali, *1980*

The Goa Gajah (Elephant Cave) sanctuary near Bedulu (Gianyar), also dating from the eleventh century, has a finely-decorated bathing place. For more than a thousand years, "heavenly water-nymphs", sculpted in stone, have been pouring thin streams of water into the rectangular pool for the glory of the gods and the purification of man. The head of a giant demon protruding from the nearby rock guards the entrance to a small cell, a rocky hermitage. Siwaite monks dwelt here in the past.

> — *Rudolf Mrazek, writing in his book* Bali, The Split Gate to Heaven, *1983.*

Bas reliefs such as the four on these pages dance, grimace, work,
pray and play on walls, gates and other architectural structures which
you'll find in all parts of Bali. These animated figures, carved out of
soft volcanic tuff stone called paras, were photographed during a
temple-hopping expedition to the Penebel area.

LIFE
As a Celebration of Itself

THE NATIVES OF BALI, ALTHOUGH OF THE SAME original stock with the Javans, exhibit several striking differences not only in their manners and the degrees of civilization they have attained, but in their features and bodily appearance. They are above the middle size of Asiatics, and exceed, both in stature and muscular power, either the Javan or the Malayu. Though professing a religion which in western India moulds the character of the Hindu into the most tame with implicit subserviency to rules and authority, and though living under the rod of despotism which they have put into the hands of their chiefs, they still possess much of the original boldness and self-willed hardihood of the savage state. Their general indifference to the oppression which they endure, their good humor and apparent satisfaction, together with their superior animation and energy, give to their countenances, naturally fairer and more expressive than those of the Javans, a higher cast of spirit, independence and manliness than belongs to any of their neighbors. They are active and enterprising, and free from that listlessness and indolence which are observable in the inhabitants of Java … What they now are it is probable that the Javans once were, in national independence as well as in religious and political institutions."

The above observations, published in Sir Thomas Stamford Raffles' *History of Java* in 1817, were made by Raffles following an 1815 visit he made to Bali. Raffles (1781–1826), the so-called "Father of British Malaya," was a keen student of social and political institutions, and he was obviously impressed by what he found on Bali. The Balinese, he wrote, "are now a rising people. Neither degraded by despotism nor enervated by habits of indolence or luxury, they perhaps promise fairer for a progress in civilization and good government than any of their neighbors." Raffles had discovered, not unlike everybody who visits this island, that the Balinese are, well, different, from other people who live in this part of the world.

Where the original Balinese — the so-called *Bali Aga* — came from is, like many other things in this place "lost in the mists of time," a matter of conjecture. Scholarly druthers and discreetly qualified comments preceded by "on the other hand" abound here.

Whether Paleolithic or Old Stone Age people lived here is uncertain. So far, no evidence from this prehistoric era has been unearthed on the island. There is an abundance of human artifacts that date to the Neolithic, or New Stone Age, but modern (or recorded) history, say from the time of Christ, is generally unknown because the oldest written Balinese sources (usually glyphs on stoneworks or Sanskrit recollections incised into copper plates or *lontar* palm-leaf books) date only from about 600 A.D. This is unfortunate, but even the oldest known Javanese stone inscriptions, on the so-called "Batutulis" near Bogor and on the "Stone of Tugu" outside what is now Jakarta, date only from about 450 A.D.

Any human activity that happened before those times, therefore, is anybody's guess and is usually allocated to a Balinese period that historians and anthropologists conveniently label "prehistory," or, in its usual breakdown, the time categories of Stone Age, Bronze Age and Iron Age (depending on how handy the Balinese became with the use of tools wrought from those three types of hard materials).

One thing we do know is that man has inhabited this part of the Indonesian archipelago for a very long time. This fact was sensationally corroborated in 1891 by the noted Dutch anatomist and geologist Eugene Dubois. During digs he made that year, Dubois (1858–1940) discovered a brainpan and thighbone at Trinil, near Java's Solo River, that were the first known fossils of the human sub-species known as *Homo erectus*. This famed Java Man, originally classified by Dubois as *Pithecanthropus erectus*, established that primitive humans lived in nearby Java as long ago as during the early and middle Pleistocene period (ca. 500,000 to 1,000,000 years ago). Dubois's discovery startled

Offerings in Bali come in a wondrous assortment of sizes and shapes. Particularly impressive are "natural" tapestries such as the huge lamak *(left) cascading down an entry gate outside a temple at Sangeh. Such* lamak *altar hangings are made of dark green sugar palm leaves and yellow-green young coconut palm leaves. Above: A Kuta woman makes an offering at the seashore.*

historians, because he proved that Java Man predated the well-known Peking Man (*Homo erectus pekinensis*) by some 500,000 years!

Given the proximity of Java, and the knowledge that at an early point in geological history the islands of Bali and Java were linked by a shallow continental shelf, it would probably be safe to assume that a Java-related Bali Man could have roamed this island's jungles, coastlines and mountains during prehistoric times.

The first "modern" or "mixed" Indonesians in this part of the archipelago are thought to have been descendants of seafaring people who migrated here from Continental Asia by way of the Indian subcontinent about 4,000 years ago, or about 2,000 B.C. They came in particular from southwest China's Yunnan province. Early language links, the designs and use of Stone Age style implements, weaving and pottery-making techniques, and the development of a wet-rice (*sawah*) style of rice cultivation support this theory.

As these Yunnanese people moved south and southwest, usually for purposes of trade, they first made contact with the coastal people of eastern India. During the next 500 years, these south Chinese and east Indian people mixed, culturally and racially. One important skill that the Yunnanese learned from the seafaring east Indians was the science of celestial navigation. This knowledge allowed them to travel and trade further south, west and east in an ever-increasing circle of exploration and influence, and by about 1,500 B.C. they reached remote landfalls such as Sumatra, Borneo, the Celebes, Java and, eventually, Bali and other parts of Nusa Tenggara. Some of the more adventurous sailed even further in search of riches — to the Spice Islands of Maluku and even as far away as New Zealand, Tahiti and (sometime between 500 and 800 A.D.) Hawaii. They carried not only trading goods, but also new ideas regarding politics, economics, agriculture and religion.

There is no way to accurately determine just how many of these Indians and Chinese settled in Bali, intermarried and added to the local proto-Polynesian gene pool, but visiting scientists have recently discovered strong evidence that Indian blood does indeed flow through Balinese veins. During 1986, a visiting medical researcher conducted blood protein tests in the village of Budakling in east Bali and found that blood samples taken from villagers there contained

what are called "India markers." Such markers, which are isolated as constituent proteins during what are called electrophoresis blood testings, are commonly found only in natives of the Indian subcontinent! It is perhaps appropriate that the name of that village — Budakling — is a combination of the local words for Buddha and Kalinga (natives of southeast India).

By the time these Chinese and Indian traders had reached Bali, however, there was already a fairly substantial population of post-neolithic people living on the island. Based on archaeological findings, these early Balinese had already evolved into a culture distinct from that of Java. They made their working implements from different kinds of stone, and they also designed and shaped them differently from those used by their Javanese cousins. These early adzes, hoes and picks are beautifully finished pieces that are now revered on Bali as important cultural heirlooms.

Among the most curious of early Balinese findings have been unusual stone sarcophagi of two distinct shapes. One of these found at Pudjungan is very short and cylindrical like a clamshell, indicating that the dead person was entombed in it in a doubled-up or squatting position. Others, like the one in the Gunung Kawi temple complex at Kaliki, look more like a proper, body-length bathtub. Both sarcophagi types were carved from single blocks of stone.

Urs Ramseyer, in his fine reference book *The Art and Culture of Bali* (Oxford University Press, 1977), reports that within such sarcophagi were found highly polished stone tools and an assortment of bronze objects, including "lances, spiral-shaped rings and bracelets, small, conical bells and heart-shaped tools with hollow shafts, which were probably used as ceremonial weapons or insignia rather than as agricultural tools. He writes, "It may be interesting to note that this bronze is not the well-known alloy of copper and tin but one of copper and about 25 per cent lead." He mentions one "artistically impressive" sarcophagus found in Pejeng in the District of Gianyar that is embellished with a high relief image of "a turtle with a projecting head and anthropomorphic traits." Many of these items described by Ramseyer can be seen in Bali's main museum in Denpasar or at the small Pejeng museum not far from the busy town of Ubud.

There is one Bronze Age object in Bali, however, that has wowed both tourists and anthropologists for centuries. This is a handsome, blue-green kettle gong, the Moon of Pejeng, which rests in a thatched-roof shrine in the inner sanctum of the Pura Penataran Sasih, an important early state temple in the District of Gianyar. This grand gong, which measures 186.5 cm long and has a sounding surface that is 160 cm in diameter, is the largest instrument of its kind in the world. It may well be the most important historical artifact on Bali. Accordingly, it is revered by the Balinese as a moon-like object that long ago fell into a nearby tree from the heavens. Myths abound about the

Balinese women have always been an important part of the island's industrious work force, whether they are involved in harvesting or clean-up campaigns (left) or spending their days minding a fruit-stand at Denpasar's central marketplace (above).

Moon of Pejeng, which, according to some estimates, may have been cast as early as 300 A.D. Archaeologists have found stone castings on Bali that were apparently used to make similarly designed gongs on Bali, but legendary stories about the Pejeng gong's celestial origins still make for a fine local legacy.

According to the anthropologist Roelof Goris, the gong was not cast directly in a stone form; rather, a sculpted stone casing was used to first make a wax model which was then covered with a fired clay; the clay mold was then heated so the wax inside would melt away. Then, in a final casting process, molten bronze was poured into this clay form to create a finished gong. Once again, there is an Indochinese connection to this hourglass-shaped gong. Such kettle gongs are found in many parts of Southeast Asia, but it is generally acknowledged that such stylized objects originated in an important Bronze Age site in Tonkin called Dong So'n. It is uncertain whether this particular specimen was made in Bali or imported, but that is of little importance to the Balinese.

Early European visitors to Bali were not just impressed by the Balinese people's artworks, sophisticated social organization and strong character, but also by their high (for those times) level of literacy. In comparison with neighboring Java and Sumatra, for example, theirs was a more highly advanced and literate society. Most conspicuous to visiting scholars was the fact that even women on Bali were often capable of reading,

writing and practicing the liberal arts. In most other Asian cultures, such learned talents were almost exclusively the province of men.

Van Bloemen Waanders, a Dutch official who visited Bali during the latter half of the 19th century, wrote to his superiors in Holland that, "It is marvelous that in a country where public schools are conspicuous by their absence and where teachers and teaching are never heard of, the knowledge of reading and writing should have attained such an extraordinary development."

Such highly developed ability is often credited to an odd turn in Indonesian religious and political history which inadvertently flooded the small island of Bali with a sudden infusion of an educated elite and ruling intelligentsia from Java. During the 14th and 15th centuries, when an agressive wave of Moslem proselytizers and conquerors poured from west to east across the Indonesian archipelago, only the island of Bali and a section of the easternward island of Lombok somehow managed to defy and repulse the spread of Islam. By dint of a series of historical accidents and fickle fate, Bali was the only one of some 13,667 Indonesian islands that remained traditionally faithful to its hybrid, Indonesian form of Buddhism-Hinduism. For some quirky reasons of their own, the newly powerful Moslems of Indonesia kept bypassing Bali, even though they swept on and converted other Sunda islands as far east as Timor and Flores.

During these times of widespread religious conver-

Indeed, business is business, whether you are dealing in mattresses, pillows and "Dutch wives" (left) or smiling at customers from behind candy and cookie jars at a neighborhood warung *(above). No matter where you go on the island, you can always find a roadside* warung *keeper eager to dispense food, drink and local gossip.*

sion, when the grand Hindu-Indonesian kingdom of Majapahit was gradually extinguished by a new Islamic empire called Mataram, thousands of persecuted Javanese-Hindus fled across the narrow Bali Strait and found religious and political refuge on Bali. With them they brought material and cultural riches. Many of the refugees who made up this brain trust were courtly aristocrats, priests, intellectuals, dancers, musicians and artists. Indeed, among them were direct descendants of the people who built great architectural wonders such as the Borobudur and the Prambanan, and who over the centuries had refined the ancient precepts of Buddhism and Hinduism into a religion (and related social and political systems) all their own.

This exodus of an intellectual elite from the vast island of Java to tiny Hindu Bali is recounted with fascination by every scholar who has ever written about this island's complicated and ironic history.

The Mexican Covarrubias wrote:

It was of extreme significance for the cultural development of Bali that in the exodus of the rulers, the priests, and the intellectuals of what was the most civilized race of the Eastern islands, the cream of Javanese culture was transplanted as a unit into Bali. There the art, the religion and philosophy of the Hindu-Javanese were preserved and have flourished practically undisturbed until today. When the fury of intolerant Islamism drove

the intellectuals of Java into Bali, they brought with them their classics and continued to cultivate their poetry and art, so that when Sir Stamford Raffles wanted to write the history of Java, he had to turn to Bali for what remains of the once great literature of Java ... .

Added the American historian Hanna:

The Balinese still share with the Javanese many common traditions of language, music, dance, sculpture and literature, but the gap between Hindu Bali and Muslim Java is almost as wide as that between youth and old age. The older, the Balinese-Majadpahit culture, paradoxically, preserved its freshness and animation [on Bali], while the younger, the Javanese-Mataram society grew both sober and somber. It is the riddle and miracle of Bali that from the embers of Madjapahit Java should have been ignited the fires which still burn bright in the neighboring islet ... .

Along with this impromptu wealth, culture and religion, these Javanese transmigrants also brought with them highly refined systems of architecture, agriculture and social organization. All of these influences are readily visible in Bali even today, but perhaps the most obvious is the ancient system of Hindu caste rankings which by birthright has for many centuries

divided the people of Bali into distinct social entities.

According to the old Balinese-Javanese Hindu four-level caste system, the highest ranking people were members of the *Brahmana*, or priestly caste. Below these brahmins came the *Ksatriya*, a ranking caste of ruling princes and nobles; then a warrior or merchant group called the *Gusti* or *Wesya* caste; and, finally, the common people, known as *Jaba* (outsiders) or *Sudra*. These days, following many years of Dutch colonization and the recent democratization of Bali by Indonesia's Jakarta-based government, such caste distinctions have been legally muted, but the Balinese still show deference to higher caste members in the way they speak to such people and, most impressively, in the way they defer to them during rituals having to with birth, adolescence, adulthood and death.

Much of this deference has to do with snobbery and social elitism, but it is an inescapable fact of Balinese life, even in this era of computers and capitalism, and even though a low caste *Sudra* may very well be many times richer than a *Brahmana* who works for him. The Indonesian government does not conduct censuses along caste lines, but it is estimated that only about 10 per cent of the Balinese belong to the *Brahmana*, *Ksatriya* and *Wesya* castes, with the remaining 90 per cent being *Sudra*, or commoners.

These days, as an emerging middle class is fast taking over positions of political and economic importance on the island, the most obvious way to determine a Balinese person's caste is to listen for his or her name. Brahmin names usually begin with the title *Ida Bagus* or *Ida Ayu*; *Ksatriyas* are addressed as *Anak Agung, Cokorde* or *Dewa*; *Wesyas* usually *I Gusti*; and *Sudras* invariably go by the first names *Wayan, Madé, Nyoman* and *K'tut*, which indicates the order in which they were born. After a *Sudra* family has used up these four first names, they simply repeat the order for their subsequent children. Because Bali's *Sudras* make up such a disproportionate part of the island's population, you will find that nine out of every ten people you meet on the island are either named *Wayan, Madé, Nyoman* or *K'tut*. This is especially disconcerting when you are lost in a large festival crowd and looking for a friend who has such a name. Yell "Madé!" out loud in the direction of a thousand or so Balinese and perhaps half the crowd will turn around, each *Madé* wondering why you are calling their name.

The most colorful and readily identifiable of these Balinese castes — particularly observed at the time of public ceremonies — are the *Brahmanas*, who are distinguished by their all-white clothing, long hair sometimes stylishly drawn up into a top-knot, and other accouterments of the priestly caste.

In keeping with the island's diverse religious rites and religious "styles," there are numerous kinds of priests on the island, each of them possessing various skills, "powers" or spiritual authority. The majority of them are the *pemangku*, who tend to regular temple

Whether at the seashore or along the shores of a mountain lake, the beat of day-to-day communal working life goes on. In one scene (left), a team of fishermen carry a gaily-painted jukung (elephant-fish canoe) up the black sands of Kusamba, and in another (above), a squad of housewives carry sheaves of rice past chilly Lake Bratan.

and community duties, but the priests' ranks also include the *dalangs*, or shadow puppeteers, and *balians*, the so-called medicine men. At the top of the island's spiritual hierarchy are high-ranking Buddhist and Hindu priests known as *padandas*, who are most visible during larger extravaganzas.

"With the exception of some seventeen brahman Buddha priests, *padanda Buddha* as they are called," writes C. Hooykaas (in *Surya-Sevana, The Way to God of a Balinese Siva Priest*, 1966), "all Balinese *padandas* (high priests) are considered to be priests of Siva … ."

The *padanda* is a priest, notes Hooykaas, "who plays a role in all elaborate ceremonies, festivities and spectacles, but who keeps himself completely aloof, and who, after an hour of murmuring and of making gestures, during which time he concentrates exclusively on himself, of throwing flowers and rice grains, of bell ringing and gesturing with the fingers, and holding cult objects above the priests' lamp (fire) and the smouldering frankincense, of splashing water which is in small containers and sprinkling it in drops, then returns home again, respected, sought out as one who prepares Holy Water, but not as one who is regarded as a leader nor followed or listened to as a preacher; as one who is unheeded and not understood. All these things are of no concern to him … ."

The above caste breakdown is generally applicable, but when traveling about Bali, one must keep in mind that it is just that, a generalization. Each of these castes is divided, in turn, into sub-castes and other social divisions. The *Brahmanas*, for example, are divided into at least five sub-groups known as *Kemenuh*, *Manuaba*, *Keniten*, *Mas* and *Antapan*, and in some places first-born *Sudras* are called *Gede* or *Putu*, second-borns are *Nengah* or *Kadek*, and third-borns are often called *Komang*. Some of this name-calling is based on logic, having to do with a particular village's evolved history or social structure, but it is also, like most other things in Bali, unexplainable and simply the way things are in a particular time, place and situation.

Two words that you will often hear regarding Balinese social groupings are *ngayah* and *makemit*. The first word, *ngayah*, refers to a group, or community, which directs its aggregate skills, work and time towards producing a traditional ceremony. The second, *makemit*, means "to guard" or "watch over," as when a group of Balinese stay all night at a temple to attend to the visiting spirits of deceased ancestors who have returned to earth for a visit.

One spectacular manifestation of Balinese group behavior that has intrigued both scholars and laymen over the centuries has to do with the ability and propensity of the average Balinese person to fall into a state of pure, hysterical trance during religious rites. Trance inducement is not so unusual in Asia — indeed, it is common to religious groups throughout the Asia-Pacific region — but in Bali it is such a commonplace phenomenon that it invites closer observation.

It's sunset time, so it's time for a daily mandi-bath (left) and a moody walk home. These late-day silhouettes were photographed in sawah plots (rice fields) located.outside the village of Batuan.

During states of trance, which almost always occur during passionate, ceremonial theater performances cum religious rituals, entranced persons become violent, thrashing and frenzied. On some occasions they babble unintelligibly. On others they cry like babies. And at still other times they assume the personae of animals and shriek like monkeys, crow like roosters or bark like dogs. To the casual, outside observer, these people are mad, possessed and "out of control" of their normal senses. To the Balinese, however, such people are momentarily blessed and occupied by higher spirits. They are *nadi*, i.e. "creative" or "existing", on a plane not too far from the gods. Consequently, entranced people (*sanghyang*) are respected and deferred to as conduits of higher spirits.

Sanghyang ceremonies are observed in many curious forms, but perhaps the most extraordinary of these rituals are the so-called *sanghyang dedari*, which feature the entranced dancing of two young girls who become possessed with the spirits of heavenly nymphs. Such *sanghyangs* are rarely held, and almost never generally publicized, because they are very important exorcism seances that are called for only when a community has experienced serious misfortune. A village that has scheduled such an exorcism may spend weeks preparing for such a ritual, centering most of its time, offerings and spiritual energy on the two *dedari*, who on the occasion of the *sanghyang* become magically possessed and perform complex dances which neither girl has ever been taught to do. According to the Balinese, no formal dance instruction is necessary because it is not the girls — but the two *dedari* goddesses possessing them — who are doing the dancing.

The Balinese doctor A. A. M. Djelantik, who is cited in an earlier chapter in this book regarding Balinese art, has long been interested in such trance phenomena — so interested, in fact, that many years ago, during his years of training to be a Western-style physician, he wrote a scholarly thesis about what he calls "the psychosis of underdeveloped people." In his thesis, Djelantik tried to explain why people from Balinese-like cultures can so easily enter a separate reality manifested by trance, while persons from Western cultures find this process difficult, if not impossible, to achieve.

In using the term "underdeveloped," Djelantik was referring to the generally non-industrialized and agrarian cultures of the so-called Third World. People in such countries, he says, have been born into and have developed character and social traits that have been heavily influenced by what he calls "strong patterns of communalism" or "impersonal group behavior."

"In such a social environment," Djelantik said, "you are so geared to communal life that this reduces the importance of your individual personality. Therefore, it is easier to lose this personality, to surpass your own individual boundaries and let go."

In the West, he says, this ability to easily let go of one's personality, or what Sigmund Freud called the

ego, has generally been lost because most westerners have a strong sense of "anxiety neurosis," or a fear of losing their personalities or "sense of self." As a result, the average Western person anxiously and aggressively clings on to his or her personality or identity to the bitter end to avoid an unpleasant "loss of ego." Consequently, this makes it very difficult, if not impossible, for such guarded persons to fall into a pure state of trance. The antagonistic muscles controlled by our brain simply rebel against such vulnerable behavior and will not allow us to relax enough to become possessed by forces outside what we perceive to be our normal state of consciousness.

In a place like Bali, however, where from birth one closely identifies with impersonal and communal behavior, this transcendental process is much easier. "Here," Djelantik says, "you will observe much more of what psychiatrists call 'hysterical neurosis,' or a state in which the loss — or giving up — of one's personality is very apparent. Because people in Bali and other undeveloped countries are more community oriented than personality oriented, they find it much easier to lose their individuality and experience true hysteria."

Such hysteria, as aforementioned, assumes many forms, depending on the ceremonial occasion during which it is induced. Perhaps the most commonly observed of these trance states are those which take place during the enactment of regular Barong-Rangda performances. At these times, as the lion-like Barong challenges the witch Rangda in a dance pitting good against evil, one commonly witnesses the chaos of trance as sometimes dozens of people are spiritually possessed and become hysterical. Some of those affected simply writhe on the ground, experiencing fits and spasms; others draw sacred kris blades from their sashes and attempt to drive these serpentining daggers into their chest or abdomen; and yet others will seize a small chicken and begin eating it alive. In the midst of all these convulsions, priests casually stroll from one entranced person to another, blessing them with holy water and chanting *sutras* until they once again return to a normal mental state. The whole effect is shocking to outside observers, but here it is considered to be a normal and logical manifestation of ritual, human behavior.

During the course of an interview, Dr. Djelantik, was asked if he had ever gone into such a trance.

"I don't have the ability to do this as intensely as my brothers," he said, "but there have been times when I have felt *outside my self.*

"When I was young, I used to dance the *baris*, and I remember that when the *gamelan* begin playing and I was up there dancing, I felt hypnotized or entranced. I experienced a sense of exhilaration that I have never really been able to explain. I don't dance anymore, but even these days I sometimes have similar feelings. If I enter certain holy places, such as the temple at Bukit, I really do feel *different* like I am no longer of this world."

Night has fallen, or is falling, so it's time to fire up kerosene lamps and conduct business in the cool of the evening air. A Singaraja lady (left) hawks posters of rock and roll and movie stars, while at a Kintamani warung (above) the glow of lamplight tempts passersby inside for a hot cup of sweet kopi Bali.

RICE TO ROYALTY
A Look at Ancestral Prerogatives

WILL RAISED HIS HEAD AND LOOKED ABOUT him. They were not far from the floor of an immense amphitheater. Five hundred feet below stretched a wide plain, checkered with fields, dotted with clumps of trees and clustered houses. In the other direction the slopes climbed up and up, thousands of feet towards a semicircle of mountains. Terrace above green or golden terrace, from the plain to the crenelated wall of peaks, the rice paddies followed the contour lines, emphasizing

every swell and recession of the slope with what seemed a deliberate and artful intention. Nature here was no longer merely natural; the landscape had been composed, had been reduced to its geometrical essences, and rendered, by what in a painter would have been a miracle of virtuosity, in terms of these sinuous lines — these streaks of pure bright colour … ."

A landscape composed? With artful intention? In this literary instance the late English author-philosopher Aldous Huxley (1894–1963) was writing about Pala, a mythical Southeast Asian island-nation where people lived a utopian existence. This island's people, the Palanese, were cooperative rice-growers with Indonesian names who had long been isolated from the outside world. The Palanese were "out of touch," but despite their isolation, they had adopted, during a period of early contact with the world outside, a curious set of social and religious beliefs that could only be identified by Huxley as a hybrid admixture of Shivaite Buddhism and "the teachings of their ancients."

The Palanese people were a handsome lot — "In the sunlight her skin glowed like pale copper flushed with rose," said Huxley of a topless Palanese woman who had walked by with a basket of fruit on her head — who because of their advanced state of agriculture were the best fed people in Asia. And because creature comforts produce leisure time, what we now call "quality time," the island of Pala, wrote Huxley "had good painting and sculpture, splendid architecture, wonderful dancing, subtle and expressive music — but no real literature, no national poets or dramatists or story-tellers. Just bards reciting Buddhist and Hindu myths; just a lot of monks preaching sermons and splitting metaphysical hairs … ."

Huxley's book about Pala, entitled *Island*, was published in 1962, a year before his death in California, and though no one has ever accused him of using the island of Bali as his model for Pala, line after line in *Island* has a familiar, *gamelan*-like ring. His observations regarding rice farming ("an affair of terracing and irrigation" that calls "for pooled efforts and friendly agreements"), for example, are peculiarly and distinctively Balinese.

"If *Brave New World* was Aldous Huxley's technological hell, *Island* was his vision of Utopia. In this, his last novel, he portrayed mankind at its sanest and most admirable," wrote Cyril Connolly, a reviewer for London's *Sunday Times*, shortly after Huxley's book about Pala was first published. Appropriately, it was similar idealistic visions of Bali's agricultural, social and religious systems that inspired many other first-time visitors to this island to write in similar, "Pala-like" bursts of socio-economic poesy.

Aernout Lintgens, who penned the first Western descriptions of Bali following its "discovery" by Dutch explorers-traders on January 28, 1597, noted in his journals that it was almost by accident that the crews of the Dutch East Indies' first three trading ships to visit Bali — the *Mauritius*, the *Hollandia* and the *Amsterdam* — put in at the island that year. That small and badly battered Dutch "fleet" was bound for further points east in a search for commercial riches, but while they were anchored off Java, near the ruins of an ancient city called Balambangan, an Indian guide-pilot, "a Gujarati named Abdul" who had joined them at Bantam, advised them to stop at a small, nearby island called Bali for fresh supplies. "He knew Bali from an earlier visit and it was his advice to call on Bali because there would be sufficient water and food [there]," wrote

Most of Bali's arable land areas, as seen from the air (preceding pages), are planted in sawah in various stages of cultivation. When the island's "staff of life" is ready for harvesting and threshing (left), everybody joins in the labor, including a grainy scarecrow image (above). Aerial photo on preceding pages is by Leonard Lueras.

Lintgens in an official Dutch account of that visit.

"That very same night — [January 28, 1597] we anchored there, and there arrived 6 messengers on behalf of the king [of Bali] who asked of us from whence we came. We said, 'From Holland.' "

The Dutch timidly proceeded to make contact with the Balinese, and to their amazement they discovered — on this and subsequent visits to the island — that Bali was not just an island rich in culture, gold and other material wealth, but, more importantly, it was the finest source of good water and foodstuffs that had yet been found in this part of the world.

Lintgens later reported to his superiors in Holland that he and other Dutchmen who visited Bali on that historic occasion were astounded at the "superfluous amount of water" on Bali. "We were surprised about the high development of the island's irrigation systems and the richness of the land as a result thereof. This island can supply surrounding countries with sufficient production because of the almost superfluous production of foodstuffs on the island. If you move through the place, in all hours you are in a village or a town where there is so much water that it is surprising. Water is run through the entire land and is led through the land to irrigate the land like the Nile River Valley in Egypt where almost never it rains like it rains here on the island of Bali." This revelation brought a twinkle to Dutch eyes, because here was *the* place — *the source* if you will — of all that a weary ship's captain

and his crew might need in this remote part of the world. Indeed, the island proved so appealing that three members of the Dutch ships' 1597 crews jumped ship to stay and bask in Bali's hospitality and riches.

More than 250 years later, explorers were still singing keen praises about Balinese agricultural techniques. "It was here," wrote the naturalist Alfred Russel Wallace in the 1850s, "that I first obtained an adequate idea of one of the most wonderful systems of cultivation in the world, equaling all that is related of Chinese industry, and as far as I know surpassing in the labor that has been bestowed upon it any tract of equal extent in the most civilized countries of Europe." Wallace recalled that he "rode through this garden utterly amazed, and hardly able to realize the fact, that in this remote and little-known island, from which all Europeans except a few traders at the port are jealously excluded, many miles of irregularly inundated country have been so skilfully terraced and leveled, and so permeated by artificial channels, that every portion of it can be irrigated and dried at pleasure… ."

Some forty years later, Captain W. Cool, a highly decorated military engineer who served extensively in the Dutch East Indies during the late 1800s, agreed in a book he wrote about Bali and Lombok that, "What cannot fail to awaken our greatest interest, next to the peculiar religion of the Balinese, is the highly developed system of their agriculture, which surpasses that of all our other islands in the archipelago."

Captain Cool, like all subsequent observers of this phenomenon, was impressed with the grand pianissimo of rice terraces he saw serpentining through broad valleys and dropping like musical chords down mountainsides, but he was particularly impressed by the elaborate social, economic, political and even religious systems that had evolved around water, land and rice during the millenia or so since the *sawah* (wet rice culture) systems had been learned by the indigenous Balinese from outside sources.

During military-related visits to Bali, Cool found himself marveling at and wondering aloud how such a "primitive" people had so perfectly banked, trenched and terraced the land, and then so meticulously constructed amazing aqueducts (both below and above ground) and dams that rivaled or bettered anything that had been constructed by the Romans in Europe or the Chinese in China.

"It is evident that for the laying out of these terraces much practice and knowledge are indispensable. The construction of the dams in the rivers necessitates hard work and abundant material; and the planting of the stakes to support the aqueducts, the preparing of all these winding mounds the whole length of the different terraces, are also very arduous labors; the apportioning of the water, which is very scarce, over all the various fields, requires continual care and supervision to prevent either accidental or intentional damage or the draining off of the water.

"It is perfectly clear," — Cool coolly concluded, "that it would be impossible for each single individual to do all this [constructing] for himself."

After much study of this engineering situation, Cool discovered Bali's *subak* system of cooperative rice-growing, a system not too different from what Huxley later described on his idealized and mythical island called Pala. The *subak*, an age-old form of Balinese unionism, or "common cause" socialism, is a cooperative that in its purest form would cause a Karl Marx or Friedrich Engels to jump for joy. Somehow, despite the powerful and sometimes greedy transgressions of a traditionally feudal ruling class, the Balinese grouped together many centuries ago to communally provide — all for one and one for all — the materials, manpower and administrative systems necessary to build and maintain irrigation systems and terraced rice fields that have got to be one of the wonders of the modern — and ancient — world.

Concepts of political and economic power, based on control of land, water and other natural or man-made resources, have come and gone in Bali over the years, but the *subak* system — and its timeless codes of distribution and conduct — have somehow endured. "The object of these institutions was to ensure to the small land-owner proportionate advantages to those enjoyed by large proprietors, without however in any way detracting from each man's individual claim," wrote Captain Cool nearly a hundred years ago, and

Once the rice has been harvested and threshed, it is then packed into cloth bags, divided among the villagers for personal needs, and then any excess stores are carried off to a cooperative market. These market-bound villagers hail from the village of Celuk (left) and the central highland town of Ubud (above).

As has been true for centuries, *nearly all agricultural labor on the island is performed manually, whether this involves plodding behind an ox plow (left), planting seedlings (top) or retilling new sawah plots (bottom). The result of such personal work are agricultural plots that are the envy of farmers in more mechanized places.*

those rights are still rigidly enforced on Bali today.

A *klian*, or elected headman, and a group of elected *subak* committee men still preside over regular *subak* meetings to oversee social, religious, technical and administrative matters regarding irrigation, planting, harvesting and other *sawah*-related matters. This *klian* can be a rich man or a poor man, depending on the politics of a particular Balinese *subak*. He can also be resident in either the "heights" or "depths" of a *subak* system, meaning at the headwaters or the lowlands, but the Balinese like to point out that the *klian* is usually a man of the lowlands. Such a man is often favored as the headman because the Balinese know, from centuries of experience, that all *subak* irrigation systems will be in good, working order if the last man to receive his fair share of water is happy.

Water is also extremely important to the Balinese for spiritual reasons. Besides providing the most important element necessary for cultivating rice, water is also "holy." Water is used in last rites to purify the soul, and is also ritually sprinkled on people, places and things as a religious blessing. Appropriately, Bali's complex religion is often referred to as *Agama tirtha*, or "the holy water religion."

Anyone who flies over Bali in a light plane or helicopter will soon be impressed by just how much of the island's available, arable land is in *sawah*, or rice paddies. Except for desert areas, craggy peaks, villages and the occasional town, nearly every part of the island that has access to water (and that is most of the island) is carpeted with rice in various stages of cultivation. It is no wonder, then, that the Balinese place such a high practical and spiritual priority on this most important of their life-sustaining commodities. Indeed, the Balinese are justifiably proud of their *nasi*.

Appropriately, yet another series of serious religious rituals have developed around the planting, harvesting and even retilling of rice fields. As usual, these very old rites differ in style from village to village.

Such observances begin with the first sprouting of seeds from ears of a preceding crop. These primary sprouts are placed in a corner of a *sawah* plot for further nurturing only on a propitious day chosen by village priests. Then, after about a month and a half, the by then matured seedlings are planted in the *sawah* only after special prayers and offerings have been made to Dewi Sri, the wife of Wisnu and the Hindu goddess of fertility. The first of these plants are ritually arranged in the rice plot's highest corner in nine geometric stools, beginning at a central point and then fanning out clockwise in order of the nine cardinal points and in the shape of an eight-pointed, magical star. "North" is always reckoned as being in the general direction of the sacred mountain, Gunung Agung.

The rice then continues to grow under the watchful eyes of the community, and at various times even more offerings are made, some to ward off pests, others to insure ongoing fertility. On the forty-fourth day after planting the crops, the villagers gather to celebrate a *sawah's* particular "feast day." Later, usually about three months after the sprouts have been placed and the new crop's first heads of rice grain have begun to appear, the rice is deemed to be "pregnant," so special palm-leaf offerings in the form of a beautiful woman, sometimes with male sexual parts, are taken to the field and placed in small shrines. These images, called *cilis*, are thought to be symbolic of either Dewi Sri or another deity, Melanting, who like Dewi Sri is also a goddess of seed, fertility and beauty. Stylized *cilis* can be seen throughout Bali, in innumerable shapes and sizes, but they almost always take the form of a tiny-waisted woman with a large, spreading headdress.

Such agricultural observances take place hundreds of times throughout the year, and are but one more example of a living, Balinese culture that is flourishing and perpetuating itself like no other on earth.

Effective control of land, water and rice crops gave rise to the island's aristocracy, or the Ksatriya caste of ruling princes and nobles. Anak Agung Gde Anom (above) is a descendant of the Karangasem court. He poses in front of a portrait of his father, who also appears in an earlier archival photo (left). Anom works as a high school teacher, but is still widely recognized and deferred to as a royal prince.

WANDERING
Through a 'Heaven' on Earth

LITTLE BOYS ARE RUNNING AROUND ON THE beach, giggling as they struggle to launch bird- and fish-shaped kites into the balmy wind. Offshore, a gaily carved and painted *jukung*, an elephant-fish outrigger canoe, is gliding across a shallow lagoon. And further out to sea, somewhere back of beyond and below a crisp horizon line of cobalt blue, a coral reef is alive with white surf and net fishermen in cone-shaped hats. Above, meanwhile, the fronds of a hundred coconut palms are

whispering, swaying like huge feather dusters that have graciously imploded. All is calm here, and that great klieg light we call the sun is doing its burning, equatorial thing.

The Wanderer, however, is prone on a straw mat, suffering from an *arak madu* hangover and waiting for the masseuse to strike.

Down come the strong brown hands of blue-bonnetted masseuse No. 82. Her scented coconut oil runs down his back, the burning sands turn everything more than two meters away into a blurred mirage, and No. 82 begins kneading life back into The Wanderer's limp and aching body. "*Bagus, B'li?*" she asks, and he simply whimpers in response. As Hemingway might have written, "It was good. There. On the sand."

Like all impromptu Bali odysseys, this one began innocently enough. The afternoon before he was simply walking down Jalan Batujimbar, making his way in the general direction of the renowned, thousand-year-old Sanur pillar, when a blue Volkswagen van screeched to a stop in front of him. "*Aduh!*" he exclaimed, because he knew at a glance that this chance meeting would mean the end of today's archaeological expedition. He knew this because the driver of the van was the born-again hedonist from Jakarta, just back from climbing Mount Rinjani on nearby Lombok island. "I think we were the first humans to kayak across Rinjani's crater lake," The Hedonist said. Then he asked with a flourish, "How about a beer?"

Three big Bintang *birs*, a pack of clove *kreteks* and two plates of *krupuk* shrimp chips later, The Wanderer and The Hedonist left the roadside *warung* and set off in the general direction of the setting sun. On the way they paused for a few minutes to marvel at the eerie music generated by a flock of swooping, trained

pigeons with small whistles attached to their necks. The pigeons provided a pleasant musical intermezzo, but hunger struck again as the sun sank into the demon-filled Java Sea.

What followed was a psychotonic fantasy: First, gossip and "super-steaks" at Madé's Warung in Kuta; then, *arak madu* after *arak madu* at Legian's open-air discotheque called Baruna; and, just before dawn, *kopi bali* with a mini-skirted Maori woman at an all-night pizza parlour known as Il Pirata. A *purnama*, a huge full moon, glowed to the west, while to the east, somewhere behind the impressive silhouette of cone-shaped Gunung Agung, morning mauves and ambers began lighting up the cloud-filled sky.

As The Wanderer and The Hedonist motored back to Sanur, moor-like mists began rising like dry ice smoke from the rice paddies, adding an almost mystical touch to the numerous temples, salt-making huts and ancestral shrines that lined the Kuta to Sanur bypass highway. Upon reaching the ancient Sanur village of Blanjong, The Hedonist, in an attempt to compensate for his diversionary tactics of the afternoon before, turned off the main paved road and onto a cobbled sidestreet. A creaking iron gate led them into a temple compound filled with weathered Shivaite demons and crumbling lingas. After a brief search, they found it — the famous thousand-year-old inscribed Sanur pillar.

This stone pillar, half-buried in a protective enclosure just behind the main Blanjong temple, was discovered in 1932 and has since been hailed as a sort of Balinese Rosetta Stone because of the clues it reveals about Bali's early Buddhist-Hindu culture. The Wanderer pulled out Kempers' handy *Archaeological Guide to Bali* and discovered that this "smooth cylindrical shaft of *paras* stone (height 177 cm, diameter 62

Art on Bali is celebrated for its function as well as form. Never mind that the sculpted waterspouts (left) are thousand-year-old nymphs. In this case, they fulfil their original purpose. Above: A detail of the odd "human" faces found on the Moon of Pejeng kettle gong. This gong is the largest instrument of its type yet found in Asia.

There are fine examples of intricate basalt sculpture everywhere on the island, but sculptural styles and motifs differ considerably, depending on the whims of local artisans. The three monster guardians (above) adorn a facade of the Pura Desa in Peliatan, a famous music and dance village located between Mas and Ubud.

cm) is crowned by a lotus cushion" and "was inscribed by the order of King (*adhipatih*) Sri Kesari Varma (*deva*) in the Saka year 835 [or] early in 914 A.D." Kempers notes that the inscription seems to refer to a military expedition against Gurun and Suwal, two mountainous countries or kingdoms that have been lost in time. Most important, however, the pillar is inscribed in two different languages — Sanskrit and old Balinese — and also in two completely different scripts — old Balinese and early Nagari. These linguistic findings, Kempers writes, "proves that an indianized settlement (kingdom) existed in this coastal region [in the early 10th century] and was comparable to previous and contemporary similar communities in West and Central Java. The early Nagari script being used especially by Buddhists suggests King Kesari was a Buddhist too."

The Wanderer and The Hedonist read this and quietly pondered its archaeological significance. With such intelligence ringing in their minds, they left, fired up the Volkswagen van, and only minutes later were back in their respective bungalows at either end of Sanur beach. "Yes, just another day in Paradise," The Wanderer said to himself as he drew the curtains in his room to keep out the morning sun and to muffle the sounds of crowing roosters and yapping peanut dogs.

Eight hours later, on the beach, masseuse No. 82 has completed her oily chore, tucked 3,000 rupiahs into her brassiere, and left The Wanderer there to roast and sleep like a sandy satay. "*Terima kasih, B'li,*" he hears her say, and with that thoughtful thank you she disappears with her beach mat and little bottle of sticky and fragrant coconut oil.

"Yes, just another day in Paradise," he says to himself again, but before he can sit up and plan his next plodding move, he is besieged by a gaggle of vendors selling magical krises, carved blowguns, silver repoussé Garuda birds and ice-cold Coca-Colas. Nearby, a stunningly topless French woman smiles, stretches back on the sand, and covers her burnt face with a paperback novel. She is pleased that the latest horde of beach salespeople have left her alone and are now hassling a woozy American who has just awakened from a deep and dream-filled sleep.

A few days and nights later our self-same Wanderer is speeding through the rolling hills of central Bali in a small Japanese land cruiser. He is touring, if you will, with a lady correspondent for America's *National Geographic* magazine. Emerald rice terraces and tiny *sawah* waterfalls are falling down a ravine to their left, and to their right a brigade's worth of waddling duck platoons are being led home by young boys bearing long bamboo poles. It's that golden hour of late afternoon when the sun's long rays pop even mundane objects into beautiful amber relief. On one side of the highway, shy, bare-breasted girls are showering themselves under gargoyle waterspouts, and in segregation across the road, village men, just in from their day's toils in the rice fields, are horsing around while

This bas relief figure of a man on a bicycle with flower blossom wheels appears on a wall of the Medrwe Karang Temple in Kubutambahan, north Bali. According to local lore, this picture was carved as a tribute to the Dutch artist-author-adventurer W. O. J. Nieuwenkamp, who in 1904 became the first Westerner to tour the length and breadth of the island of Bali on a bicycle.

enjoying their late afternoon *mandi*, or freshwater bath. Bali is wonderful at this time of the day, but the much-traveled lady correspondent is obviously jaded.

"Yes, Bali is a beautiful place," she sighs, "but I must say that it really hasn't knocked me out the way I expected it would."

Slightly startled by her comment, The Wanderer turns his gaze from the passing motion picture that is Bali, and asks: "Really? It hasn't knocked you out? That being the case, what other island in the world would you recommend as being better? Where else have you found this much physical beauty and cultural activity in one small island place?"

She thinks for a while, then replies with a shrug: "I guess you're right. There is no other place quite like Bali. And to answer your question, I really can't think of another island that is as culturally alive as this one."

Only about three more minutes down the road, her jet-set boredom is relieved as the 4-wheel-drive vehicle approaches an intersection somewhere between Bugbug and Bangbang. On both shoulders of this country road appear scores of Balinese people of all ages in full ceremonial drag. A marching bronze *gamelan* is pounding out a festive, resonant composition, and perhaps a hundred women decked out in their finest *kains* and *kebayas* stroll along like ramp models with meter-high offerings baskets balanced neatly on their perfectly postured heads.

"Stop! Follow those sarongs!" yells the lady corres-

pondent, and the Balinese driver moves with the parade's easy-going flow down a bumpy side road. A kilometer or so later the two writers and their driver happen upon a crowd of people milling around the entrance to a large village temple. In any other part of the world this would have been cause for great journalistic or anthropological excitement, but on Bali such out-of-the-way festival finds are normal fare. Indeed, since leaving busy Denpasar town, this is not the first, but the fourth such ceremony that the two travel writers have encountered on what was to have been a leisurely drive to Karangasem.

The driver asks a young boy what is going on, and he is told that the village is observing a pre-Galungan temple anniversary, or *odalan*, inside the local *pura puseh*, where grand offerings are being made in honor of the village's ancestors.

"Well, why not," the lady correspondent says with a resigned smile, and inside the temple she and The Wanderer spend the next two hours before darkness enjoying a backwoods medieval pageant that rivals anything that could be produced on a Broadway stage. In one corner of the *pura puseh*, streams of women arrive every minute or so and pile huge, intricately designed fruit and floral *banten* onto an offerings pavilion. And in another sacred quarter, a team of white-robed *padandas*, or high priests, wearing red turbans and sacred amulets, prays before a lavish ancestors' altar full of painted *barongs*, opium pipes and other primitive heraldry peculiar to this part of the island. As the priests chant in sonorous tones and wriggle their hands through a series of ancient gestures called *mudras*, some in their number would now and then leap from the ground and enter that frenetic state of mind called trance. Racked with convulsions, these possessed people would chatter like monkeys, babble like birds, or simply jabber away in unintelligible tongues. Some would draw a kris from their sash, go wild-eyed and shudder as they try to drive the dagger's point into their abdomen. When this would happen, cool-minded friends would grab the entranced person's body and wait for one of the presiding priests to cool him or her down with ritual prayers and sprinklings of holy water. Through it all, children coo in their mothers' arms, little mongrel dogs poke around and eat little rice offerings, and everybody continues to celebrate, as if nothing untoward is

going on. It is a strange ritual chaos punctuated by absolute calm and casual indifference.

The Balinese driver informs his charges that this particular temple ceremony would probably continue until dawn the next day. Next on the evening's agenda, he says, is a sacred *rejang* dance, which would be followed, in turn, by *topeng* mask plays and an important all-night *wayang kulit calonarang* shadow puppet play. As he relates that local cultural intelligence, a group of elderly women, also seemingly in trance, emerges from the crowd and begins swirling through the compound in the strong, dervish-like movements of a *pendet* offerings dance. One of the village *gamelans* assembled for the occasion hammers out a frenetic score in accompaniment, and the lady correspondent and The Wanderer soon find themselves showered in frangipani blossoms tossed into the air by the whirling *pendet* dancers.

"I simply don't have the energy to see any more," the lady correspondent says an hour later. "My mind has been drained of any remaining ability to pay proper attention." So, as the *gamelan* bursts into a new overture, the two journalists depart from the temple, walk away through fireflies flitting about in the darkness, and leave that remote village to its ritualistic devices.

"What is the name of that place? Where were we?" the lady correspondent asks several kilometers later. "I don't know. I forgot to ask," says The Wanderer. The driver instinctively heads back towards Denpasar and their homes in Sanur. It isn't where they meant to go, but after all that had happened, it didn't seem to matter that they never did reach Karangasem.

Following a humid, dream-filled sleep, The Wanderer awakes with a start. A muffled, faraway explosion is rattling the windows of his bedroom and has caused a monkey in the neighboring compound to run *amok*. Outside, people are yelling, chickens are scattering, and the monkey is hysterical. It's a beautiful day, but all is not calm in the "Morning of the Earth."

Perhaps fifteen minutes later, the monkey is still going bananas, and the mud-walled compound next door is in chaos. The Wanderer's *pembantu* (maid) informs him that the monkey has bitten a gardener and is now threatening yet other humans. In response, people are shouting unkindly epithets in Balinese, brandishing bamboo poles for protection, and driving the poor monkey into a greater state of dementia.

Suddenly, two loud bangs ring out, so The Wanderer and his *pembantu* race to the second floor window just in time to see a member of the local *polisi* constabulary fire off two more rounds from a large and shiny revolver. The gun is clutched in two hands held at arm's length, and the officer is aiming in the direction of a quavering palm tree. Finally, on a fifth try, he nails the *gila* (crazy) monkey. The poor little fellow screams one last primeval scream and drops to the ground with a dull thud. The neighbors cheer, the gendarme holsters his trusty six-gun, and The Wanderer goes

When the sun is high, it's time to lay back and wait for a cooler time of day (left). Above: Curious visitors explore the monumental ruins of Gunung Kawi, the "Poet's Mountain" on the eastern banks of the Pakerisan River near Tampaksiring. These five candis, hewn out of solid rock, are "Royal Tombs" which date to the 11th century A.D.

back to sleep. The Law has restored Calm and Order.

A few hours later, over late morning *kopi* and black rice pudding, The Wanderer finds out through the village "Coconut Wireless" gossip network that the monkey was spooked into his madness by visiting French President François Mitterrand's Concorde jet as it broke the sound barrier over nearby Java. Mitterrand's two-day Bali holiday had ended, and in the quiet village of Sanur a little monkey named Bagus had died.

Later that day, The Wanderer motorcycles to Kuta Beach on the opposite side of the Bukit Peninsula to watch the passing scene at Madé's Warung. At this little bohemian cafe just down Kuta's main street from "Bemo Corner," tropical boulevardiers sit around in little clutches, stirring clouds into their coffee, comparing fashion designs, and, now and then, glancing at the main, open-air entrance to see who will walk in next. Madé herself holds forth at a non-existent cash register, and back in the kitchen sits her mother, saronged and topless, chopping up vegetables. Wrought-iron Dutch lamps hang over marble-topped tables and esoteric jazz riffs pour out of loudspeakers.

Around those marble-topped tables, Bali's beautiful people, who look like post-modernist hippies in their Kuta-style fashion ensembles, yawn, gossip animatedly and exchange odd bits of travel intelligence about parties, discotheques and *real* barong dances. In one quarter, five cheesecake-eating surfer-boys from Brazil hoot and holler as they describe the waves they rode during their latest surfari to G-Land (Grajagan Bay) in east Java. "The tubes were primo," says one. And in another corner, three morose French women compare tans and sniff at the Australian wine they have just been served. Outside, on the sidewalk, a little Balinese boy is hawking copies of yesterday's *Bali Post, Indonesia Times* and the *International Herald-Tribune*.

News of the outside world is voraciously read by most transient expatriates, but after one has been in Bali long enough, stories about attempted coups in Thailand, Wall Street stock scandals and the Iran-Contra political scams begin to diminish in importance. What begins to matter is the kind of news stories you read about in the daily *Bali Post*.

The ambience at Madé's is a bit too existential on this particular afternoon, so The Wanderer hides away at a back table with a cappuccino and the weekend *Bali Post*. In those pages he finds out:

• That Denpasar housewives are beginning to complain that "servants now want salaries that are higher than before." One disgruntled matron is quoted as being upset because housemaids are demanding 20,000 rupiahs (about US$14) a month or twice what they were being paid last year.

• That in Singaraja, a recent hotbed of scandal, local police authorities are investigating a kitchen murder allegedly provoked by black magic. The 70-year-old female victim in this homicide case was accused by relatives of being a *leyak*, or witch.

The long coastal road west of Singaraja is distinguished by its tall trees that create cool, sun-dappled tunnels for local pedestrians and bicyclists (left and above) and faster moving motorists. The effect is a "north Bali" mood quite different from what one feels when driving across other geographical zones on the island.

According to them, she was upsetting the equilibrium of her village, so "to clear the air," they killed her.

• That in central Bali, local farmers are now successfully raising a new breed of saddleback pigs imported from Australia. In this article, an animal doctor explains how you can mate the imported pig with a regular Balinese pig and how you can test the pig to determine whether or not she is pregnant.

Meanwhile, a television columnist announces that the three big American shows being aired on Bali T.V. this season will be "Charlie Angels," "The A-Team" and "CHIPS" (a serial about the California Highway Patrol); a medical advice column notes that the Denpasar General Hospital cannot do plastic surgery; and a sports item lists the latest winners of a bowling tournament held this past week at the Bali Beach Hotel.

Bowling in Bali? You bet, and once you grow weary of strikes and spares, you can repair to a poolside lounge for a Baliburger and a Bali High rum drink that is served in a bamboo tube and topped off with a tiny pink parasol stuck into a wedge of sliced pineapple.

Bowling, Baliburgers and little pink parasols are not The Wanderer's thing, so after catching up on local news and people-watching at Madé's Warung, he strolls down to Kuta's surf-pounded beach and joins other Paradise-seekers who have gathered there to ritually watch the sun set into the Java Sea. "Oohs" and "ahs" ripple through this evening's gaggle of sun worshipers as the big orange globe in all its full glory makes its way beneath the darkening horizon.

On the way back to Kuta's main street, The Wanderer nostalgically recalls what this little fishing village was like 15 years ago. Today, Kuta is something of a Hindu-Balinese Tijuana, chock-a-block with crowded discotheques, blaring sound systems, blinking neon lights, electric streetlamps and innumerable restaurants, *losmens* and retail shops with trendy names. But back in early 1972, about two years after commercial jet aircraft began landing at nearby Ngurah Rai Airport, there wasn't much going on here. In those days, most moneyed visitors stayed in hotels and bungalows in Sanur (Bali's original beach resort), Denpasar or Ubud. Kuta, meanwhile, was where low-budget "hippies" and traveling surfers found peace, brotherhood, uncrowded surfing waves and little eating spots that sold potent magic mushroom omelettes "guaranteed to last for at least four hours." All evening business here was conducted under flickering lamplight, none of Kuta's side streets were paved or illuminated by streetlamps, and sunset time on the beach was the psychedelic — "far out, man" — climax to an energetic day spent hallucinating under the influence of psilocybin. If you wanted to boogie in Bali back then, you did it in your own bungalow to the accompaniment of a battery-powered tape recorder; or, better yet, you danced flirtatiously with village virgins at an occasional *joged* dance party.

Nowadays, Kuta's main street has sprawled north-

wards like a little thatch-and-bamboo Las Vegas strip, engulfing, in the commercial process, the neighboring villages of Legian and Seminyak. At Seminyak, several kilometers down the road, you will find Chez Gado Gado, the island's most chic discotheque, and probably the only disco in the world that advertises being open only on Fridays, Saturdays *and* full moon nights.

The scenes one encounters on the road between Kuta and Seminyak would turn former Bali romantics such as Covarrubias and McPhee in their graves. After all, they never got to see a parade of Kuta Cowboys, replete in *topeng* masks, Texas boots, leather jackets and greasy jeans, roaring down the street in a Harley-Davidson motorcycle parade. Nor did they ever get to visit the Pink Panther Bar & Disco where long-haired local boys bebop under strobe lights with traveling salesgirls from Madura and Surabaya. Indeed, shop signs of the times flash by in a dizzying blur, advertising, among other delights and diversions, The Rum Jungle, Baik-Baik Boutique, Easy Rider Tours & Travel, Il Pirata Pizzeria, Piranha Dive Shop, Komodo House of Leather and the Mrs. Apple Warung.

Meanwhile, at the Peanuts Club Discotheque, perhaps 500 rowdy Australians, nearly all of them decked out in their national costume of shorts, rubber slippers and cotton singlets, have gathered to drink beer and cheer on the contestants in tonight's weekly banana-eating contest. A sign in the club proudly notes that "All Bananas Are Provided Free by the Management." "Tomorrow Night, At The Casablanca Bar," another sign notes, "Join Us For Our Weekly Wet T-Shirt and Beer-Drinking Contest."

It's almost too much to bear, so The Wanderer steals down a dark side street and spends the rest of this evening in Kuta drinking margaritas and eating tacos at T.J.'s Cantina on Poppies' Lane.

The next morning, it's time, once again, to *makan anging* (literally, "eat wind") — which is what Indonesians say when they take off and travel with no particular goal in mind — so The Wanderer wakes up, showers, and heads down to Sanur's main street to catch a *bemo* ("motorized *becak*" taxi) bound for the cool and calm of the Balinese interior.

"*Badung! Badung!*" yells an approaching *bemo* conductor, so The Wanderer climbs in and heads toward Denpasar (or Badung as it's traditionally called). Climbs in is the only way to express this act, because inside the crowded *bemo* he has to negotiate a bound pig, four chickens tied together at the ankles, and an odd assortment of bamboo baskets filled with market goods. "*Tarik!* (Let's Go!)," the *bemo* boy yells, and the little taxi van speeds off.

About six kilometers down the road, the *bemo* pulls into Stasiun Kereneng, so it's time to transfer to an even larger *bemo*, this time bound for Ubud. From Kereneng to Ubud, the *bemo* roars through a familiar string of towns and villages: first, Batubulan and its stone carvers cum *barong*-dancers; then, the silver-

Once again, the Bali mood varies dramatically. One afternoon you can marvel at the sight of a saltworker carrying seawater up a steep black sand beach at Kusamba (left), and the following morning you can inhale cool mountain air and watch the morning scene as it is reflected on the mirror-like waters of Lake Bratan, (above). Following pages: West Bali's Tanah Lot temple in sunset silhouette.

smiths of Celuk, followed by the artists of Batuan-Sukawati, the woodcarvers of Mas, the dancers of Peliatan, and, at journey's end about an hour later, the cool highland of Ubud. "Stop-ah!" The Wanderer calls, and he hops out of the *bemo* — frazzled but none the worse for wear — in front of Ubud's royal palace.

Just down the street, at Ubud's Cafe Lotus, two leering *naga* dragons and an angst-filled turtle stare stonily from their sculpted pedestals at upmarket travelers who are enjoying *crêpes américaines,* infusion coffee and homemade fettuccine *al fresco.* On the opposite side of a large pond choked with rising pink lotuses sits the impressive Pura Kamuda Sari, a palatial temple designed by Ubud's late master artist-architect I Gusti Nyoman Lempad. Classical music pours out of the cafe's sound system and the sweet smells of frangipani and freshly-baked carrot and cashew nut cake entice passersby off Ubud's busy main street. Indeed, what we have here — in Ubud and neighboring Campuan — is a sort of bamboo Aspen, a chic little hill station bursting with art galleries, trendy eating spots and thatched roof chalets-for-hire.

The Wanderer, irrepressible boulevardier that he is, is sitting under a blossom-filled trellis, exchanging small talk with Rio Helmi, the Cafe Lotus' Sumatran-Turkish proprietor. Helmi has just said goodbye to a group of tourists who had motored up to Ubud for a day of lunch and "package tour" sightseeing.

"Sometimes I meet some really interesting tourists," says Helmi, "but sometimes" — and he sighs as he says this — "I get tired of hearing the same nice things over and over again. You can only listen to people telling you how beautiful Bali is for so long before it starts to seem strange."

As Helmi says that, three blue-haired women from Australia walk in and begin clucking over the lotus pond. "Isn't that a beaut! Just look at that funny monster over there, Mabel!" shrieks one of the ladies, and Helmi once again (this time with emphasis) *sighs*.

Outside, in the dust of traffic, little boys crowd around tourists, trying to make eye contact and negotiate the sale of lurex sarongs, hand-carved chess sets, winged goddesses, and even, if you can dig it, bananas to feed to the naughty monkeys that harass visitors during their tours of a nearby monkey forest.

Such monkey business is not the norm on the island of Bali, but it and other unusual economic situations should be seriously considered when one is on tour here. Laws of supply and demand are profitably observed in Bali, and are generally ruled by a situation-to-situation business ethic that is karmically expressed as, "My good luck, your bad luck."

Night had fallen, and sleepy Ubud town was enveloped in quiet darkness, so The Wanderer wearily trudged up to Campuan and made his way up a long stairwell that led to the Beggar's Bush, Ubud's only late night pub. At the Beggar's Bush (London, 1415–1679; Ubud, 1979–   ), 1930s jazz riffs filled the air,

providing background music for a group of young Balinese cowboys who were busy hustling Australian tourist chicks at the main bar.

"*Satu arak madu*," The Wanderer said to the barkeeper, then he disappeared to a corner table to enjoy his nightcap and review the odd collection of field notes he had gathered during the past few weeks.

As he sifted through the various bits of ink and paper that had accumulated in his rucksack, The Wanderer wondered to himself just what people Out There would be interested in reading about Bali. Indeed, on an island like this, where the people mount perhaps 10,000 or more religious festivals a year, and where colorful characters of every ilk and nationality pass through one's life daily, what really becomes important and worthy of documentation?

What would gourmets think about the toasted dragonflies that Balinese children like to munch on during the Galungan-Kuningan festival season? Or what would anthropologists say about the "straw men" of Trunyan, who don *topeng* masks, big, grassy capes, and then walk through that village and lash out at people with a big whip?

On one sheet of paper entitled "Fashion note: What would they think about this in Paris?" The Wanderer referred to a "Balinese hairstyle note" gleaned from author Hickman Powell's *The Last Paradise* (1930). In a sequence about an *arja* dance concert he had attended, Powell described the *haute coiffure* of a

Balinese friend named Chetig: "One night I saw him at the *arja* play all dressed up, but instead of a flower or so in his hair … he had entangled a dozen fireflies, that shone on and off in the dark throughout the entire evening." Now what would the punks in Queens think about that? The Wanderer thought.

His favorite found quote, however, was a simple, satirical poem that was allegedly written in the 1930s by Noel Coward in the complaints book at Denpasar's old Bali Hotel. After touring Bali, and sampling her much-publicized charms, Coward commented:

> As I said this morning to Charlie
> There is far too much music in Bali
> And although as a place it's entrancing
> There is also a thought too much dancing
> It appears that each Balinese native
> From the womb to the tomb is creative
> And although the results are quite clever
> There is too much artistic endeavor.

A few days later, back home in Sanur, The Wanderer found himself sitting at the seaside, scribbling away again, trying to remember even more local trivia he had collected during his past 18 months here. After an earnest hour or so of such mental collating, he looked up from his notes, raised a cool gin-and-tonic to his lips, and smiled as Gunung Agung once again revealed itself across the sea. It was about an hour before

Busy Denpasar town is sometimes chaotic, but also lots of fun, whether you enjoy riding behind the jingling bells of a horse-drawn dokar taxicab (left) on busy Jalan Gajah Mada, or laughing with a group of Balinese boys (above) outside the town's fine Museum Bali.

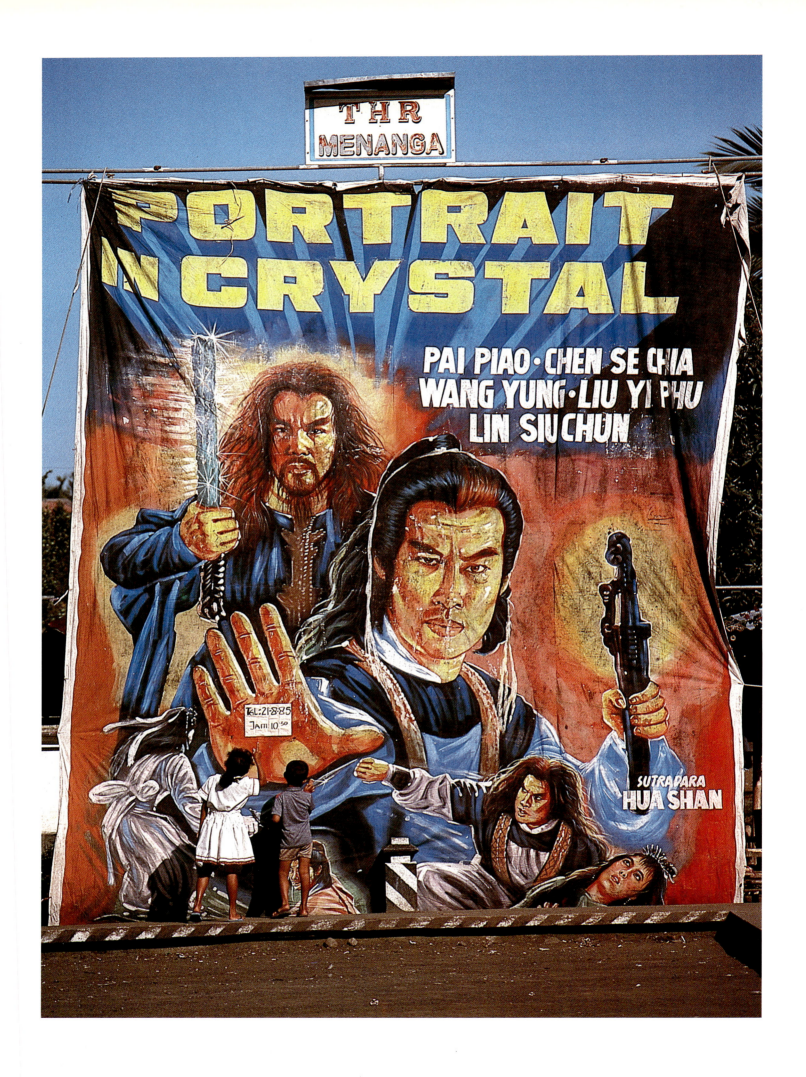

Sukawati cup.
TGL. 3 % 11 JULI 1985

sukawati
cup VIII

PEMUDA SUMBER DAYA INSANI PEMBANGUNAN

sunset, and the thick daytime haze that usually obscures that distant and sacred mountain had settled around its wide base like a smoke ring. The mountain's swollen breast rose triumphantly above Bali's east coast highlands, beaches and the placid reefs and waters off sleepy Sanur.

"Wouldn't it be marvelous," he wrote in his notebook, "to be sitting here, by the poolside at the hotel Tandjung Sari, enjoying a tall drink, when that mountain begins blowing its top?" He tried to imagine its awesome presence, reflected in the glassy Sanur lagoon, as huge jets of fire and smoke exploded into the sky and poured over the volcano's steep slopes. The Wanderer had witnessed many other volcanic eruptions in progress — on the Big Island of Hawaii and in parts of central and east Java — so he knew, like every other human who has ever humbly comtemplated such primeval activity, that volcanoes are indeed The Greatest Show on Earth. *Nothing* is more hypnotic, awesome and godly than the noisy and brilliant specter of such an eruption roaring and spouting before your eyes in an act of Creation.

That mother up there could pop any minute, he thought to himself. And as his remaining days on Bali drifted by, he became more and more curious about the mountain. Every morning and evening he would see his Balinese neighbors pray and make offerings in the general, sacred direction of Gunung Agung, and every time that would happen he would turn to the object of their spiritual energy and watch it — in his mind's eye — as it blew bright fire into the heavens.

It occurred to him each time this fantasy took place that the ultimate pilgrimage on this island of non-stop pilgrims would be a ceremonial hike to the top of that sheer volcano. After all, that mountain is the axis or directional rosette around which the Balinese universe spins, so he was determined to go up there and check it out himself. Very few of his Balinese friends had ever been up there, so he didn't know what to expect. "It's a very special place. Different from the rest of Bali," said one person who had been there, and this only piqued The Wanderer's curiosity the more.

Finally, on a relatively clear morning that seemed auspicious for mountain climbing, he and an American friend who had lived on Bali for many years (but had never been Up There), decided to make their first hike to the "Navel of the Universe." They had planned to make this expedition for a few weeks, but the weather was always uncooperative. Before setting off in the direction of the mountain, however, they consulted Balinese friends and prepared, as the Balinese would, for their ascent to the realm of Sanghyang Widi Wasa. Along with food, water and warm clothes, they packed small *banten* offerings, sticks of incense, temple sarongs and sashes, and empty plastic bottles so that they could bring back holy water from Tirtha Mas, the sacred water cache near the summit.

When they were about to leave, Rawi, The Wanderer's

Two of the island's favorite leisure time activities have to do with sports and movies. Once again, local artists are recruited to advertise what's happening, as evidenced by these hand-painted billboards for a martial arts movie being shown at Menanga (left) and a big soccer tournament taking place off the main road in Sukawati (above).

doting *pembantu*, warned him: "Be careful up there. Remember to talk only about good things. "Don't say bad things." She then went to the small *padmasana* shrine on the mountain side of their living compound and made yet another offering to the mountain spirits.

Off they sped in a small pick-up truck, and perhaps an hour and a half later, after a last half hour of bumping and shaking up a rock-strewn country road, The Wanderer and his friend were in the small village of Sorga. The place name Sorga means "Heaven," and it seemed somehow appropriate to be using Heaven as a starting point for a hike to the center of the universe.

From this highland village, you can see for many kilometers to the south and west of Bali, all the way to Sanur, Nusa Dua and the airport at Tuban, and across the Badung Strait to the offshore island of Nusa Penida. It is the last point where humans cultivate the land on this side of the mountain, and the people who live in the cold up here are a tough and hardy lot who cheerfully scratch out an existence in recently deteriorated lava flows. Below Sorga is another village of rugged survivors called Sebudi.

During the devastating 1963 eruption of Gunung Agung, when the whole world around here was caving in, most of the villagers of Sebudi gathered in their main temple next to the village school. As the fiery mountain gods above them roared, the villagers hastily made offerings, priests began praying like they had never prayed before, and *gamelan* musicians began pounding out ancient refrains. It was a last ditch effort to appease the wrathful spirits above.

"Everybody was in the *pura*, making offerings and asking for protection of the gods," recalled a man of Sorga. "Then a big *lahar* (a wave of hot, volcanic mud) hit the temple, knocked it over and swept everybody away. Until today, nobody has ever found either the villagers, the musicians or the *gamelan*."

With that story about this mountain in mind, the two hikers entered Sorga's biggest temple, sat on the ground under a big *waringin* (banyan) tree, and took part in a first offering ceremony. *Bantens* and money were placed into a shrine, incense was burned and waved in the air, flowers were tossed to the gods, and the senior of the two guides ritually sprinkled the visiting Americans with holy water. That first ritual completed, the hikers set off on the first leg of the zig-zagging trail to the top of Gunung Agung.

The first hour or so was spent humping up and down misty ridgelines and gullies that grew more hot and humid with every heavy step. Even at this early stage of the hike, gravity was adding uncomfortable weight to bodies and backpacks, and sweat dripped from their brows onto the ground. After what seemed like miles and hours, they reached station number two, a spectacular temple site called Pasar Agung. At this ancient place, dark, fiber-topped *meru* roofs and rough, stone-cut shrines rose in a clearing above a large *marae* built with thousands of black lava stones.

It's amazing how many tourists pack light for a trip to Bali, then head home with a hand-carved banana plant (above) or garuda bird (right) as part of their baggage. Though carving was traditionally a craft used almost exclusively to produce ritual objects, the Balinese have learned during this century to adapt to the eclectic tastes of visiting souvenir hunters from all parts of the world.

The piled-on stone construction of this pyramidal temple platform reminded The Wanderer of Hawaiian *heiaus* (temples) erected in much the same way.

At Pasar Agung, under a fine Vishnu image housed inside a seven-roofed shrine, offerings were once again made. Incense burned, holy water was sprinkled, and the climb resumed. As the four pilgrims left Pasar Agung, afternoon clouds cleared and they saw the impressive hard rock summit of Gunung Agung for the first time since leaving Sorga. It seemed so close, up there above the tree and cloud lines, but everybody knew it was still far away. Next stop: Tirtha Mas, the sacred holy water site called "Gold Water." One of the Balinese guides warned them that Tirtha Mas should be reached "before the sun drowns," so that a sleeping encampment could be established below the tree line.

Tirtha Mas, which is really more of a mossy and dank sump than the golden, babbling spring one expected to see, was finally reached about an hour and a half later, after a last clamber over a slippery rock shelf. Evidence of former visitations, in the form of garishly painted graffiti and Indonesian names, covered the many boulders that protect this sacred waterhole. Again, in keeping with local protocol, yet more offerings were made, more money and incense placed, and even more holy water sprinkled on everyone's head.

This cool holy water site sits just above the mountain's prevailing cloud line and about 100 meters below its tree line, so it is the last decent spot to camp

out for the night — and before making the last two-hour assault to the top of this huge crater. That night, above shifting clouds and the distant lights of Karangasem, the four pilgrims huddled around the flames of a bonfire, contemplated the millions of stars that filled the impossibly clear sky above them, and listened to the surf-like rustle of the bitingly cold wind as it rushed through Gunung Agung's last trees.

The next morning, perhaps a half hour before sunrise, they began their final, sleepy assault up the volcano's ever-steepening cone.

Beyond the tree line, under the fading moonlight, the landscape changed dramatically. What was once earth now was the moon, and the mountain grew eerily silent. Except for the sound of volcanic cinder stones crunching underfoot, the mood was that of a huge, deserted vacuum chamber. Below stretched a vast, cottony mattress of clouds that began turning pink and then salmon as the sun began rising to the east; above, meanwhile, glowered strange, jutting rock forms that were spewed into haphazard positions during the historic 1963 eruption.

Up a ragged ridge line the four mortals trudged, breathing heavily in the thin air and counting each leaden step. The going was slippery, and whenever somebody would fall, or send a stone careening down a slope, the elder of the two Balinese guides would put a finger to his lips and whisper, *"Awas, Tuan,"* not because he was worried about the people in his charge, but because he was concerned that too much noise might awaken and anger the sometimes destructive gods who were sleeping Up There.

As dawn brightened and began warming up the volcano's eastern flank, its dark side remained a dark metallic blue that faded into a monochromatic forest green and the foggy white of shifting cloud banks below. "These two Balinese guys have never been in an airplane, but being up here they already know what it feels like to fly Garuda," said The Wanderer's friend.

Straight up, or at least on a 45 to 55 degree angle that felt like straight up, was the top. Again, the summit looked close, but in this rarified environment everybody knew it was still achingly far away. Every turn and climb led to one more optical illusion just beyond reach. The only audible sounds were those of gasping lungs and one's own throbbing pulse. Every hundred meters or so, the weakest excuse was excuse

enough for a rest stop and yet another lingering look at the island's best view. Yes, Bali high: Somewhere over there is Lombok, and in the opposite direction was the rising cinder cone of Gunung Batur.

A last heart-pounding trail ran along and up a crumbling ridge that looked like the back of a sleeping dinosaur. The foot path grew increasingly precarious, and on either side of this tricky rise were frozen rivers of black and rust-colored lava, gorges strewn with huge mangled boulders, and topsy-turvy slabs of burgundy and amber tephera.

The plodding ascent continued, and finally, after carefully crawling hand by foot around and over a last monster rock, they could see it — the crater's rim. "I don't believe it. There really is a summit," said The Wanderer, and they all stopped to meditate on the final, rock-covered grade that rose ahead of them.

Every counted step to the top was a killer, every breathless turn of the head a zen meditation, and when they ultimately reached the less than two meters wide niche that marks the top of the volcano, they sat down once again to catch their breath before looking into the crater. Sulphurous gases, emitted by steam vents on the crater floor, made this difficult.

"I'm afraid to look," said The Wanderer.

"After all that we've been through, we have to look," smiled his friend.

They carefully pulled themselves up the last few feet, propped themselves against two big rocks on the

volcano's crumbling rim, and gazed into a grand caledera that took their breath away. "*Aum Swastiyasu,*" The Wanderer said to himself, and he blinked to assure himself that he really was up here at the very brink of that which is holiest to the Balinese.

The crater's interior walls were disoriented, twisted and chaotically rearranged patterns of rust, yellow and gray-black, a Byzantium mosaic that had been scrambled by higher forces into an impossible puzzle. It was a new but at the same time prehistoric place different from any other they had seen on Bali.

Between them, in the saddle of the small observation niche, were scattered remnants of other climbers' offerings — small clay figurines, Chinese *kepeng* coins, dried bananas and flowers, and scattered rice and beans that had been shaken out of bamboo tubes. It was a simple but important little altar.

The two Balinese guides were getting cold, nervous and impatient. They didn't like being up there, so close to the spirits of their ancestors, so they inched their way up the slope to the two Americans with two last sticks of incense and what remained of their *banten* offerings. The incense was lit, the *bantens* were placed on the small, makeshift altar, and the two foreigners were urged to say their last — and most important — prayers of the journey.

The Wanderer and his friend complied, held their hands up for a last splash of holy water, and reluctantly set off on the long hike back down to "Heaven."

At sunny Kuta by the sea, convention is tossed to the winds. Toplessness and especially uncovered thighs (left) are frowned upon by local authorities and residents, but flaunted by sun-worshiping visitors. Above: Another brand of hedonism sizzles on the hot sands of popular Kuta Beach. Following pages: The marbled interior of Bali's sacred Gunung Agung. Photo by Leonard Lueras.

These superb traditional topeng masks were carved by the late Ida Bagus Gelodog, a master mask carver from the village of Mas. The top-center mask is that of the supreme Rajah of Majapahit, while in the middle and bottom rows are masks of a lower ranking Rajah of Klungkung (middle left) and a group of court ministers and advisers.

APPENDICES

A MAP OF THE ISLAND

HISTORICAL CHRONOLOGY

DISCOGRAPHY

FILMOGRAPHY

BIBLIOGRAPHY

INDEX

ACKNOWLEDGEMENTS

BALI

- ◉ CAPITAL
- ● CITY
- • VILLAGE

━━━ MAJOR HIGHWAY
━━━ PROVINCIAL ROAD
--- PROVINCE BOUNDARY
∧ MOUNTAIN PEAK
▨ REEF
� PLACES OF INTEREST

JAVA SEA

Menjangan Island

Apatagung

② GILMANUK

Kelatakan ∧

Merbuk ∧   Musi ∧

Mesche ∧

Patas ∧

① BANYUWANGI

Melaya

JEMBRANA

BALI

NEGARA ●
③
Pesantren

S. Daya River

MENDOYO ●

Pengambengan

Prancak

Air Satang

Pulukan ●

Seririt ④
Bubunan
PENGASTULAN
Ringkidik
Pulaki

STRAIT

JAVA

Inset map (Southeast Asia): Thailand, Kampuchea, Vietnam, Burma, Philippines, Malaysia, Brunei, Singapore, *Pacific Ocean*, INDONESIA, Papua New Guinea, **Bali**, *Indian Ocean*, Australia

Scale:
0 1 2 3 4 5 10 15 20 25 30 miles
0 1 2 3 4 5 10 15 20 25 30 35 40 45 50 kilometers

BALI

Manoa Mapworks

GIANYAR

Sukawati:	– Classical *wayang* theater village
Batuan:	– Classical music, art, dance and carvers' village
Blahbatuh:	– Site of Pura Gaduh, temple dedicated to 14th century leader Kebo Iwa
Mas:	– Woodcarvers' village, dating to 15th century *rahmanas*
Bedulu:	– Pre-Gajah Mada Balinese monarchy, ca.1343
Pejeng:	– Site of the *Moon of Pejeng* drum, a 4th century cast-bronze masterpiece
Ubud:	– Fine arts and music village; tourist and student hub
Gunung Kawi:	– Monastic complex of *stupas* and monks' cells, ca. 11th century
Tampaksiring:	– Site of Tirta Empul public spring baths, built ca. 962 A.D.

BANGLI

35.	**Penulisan:**	– Site of Pura Tegeh Koripan, Bali's highest situated temple
36.	**Kintamani:**	– Earliest known kingdom, 10th century; 1500m above Lake Batur
37.	**Gunung Batur:**	– Much revered volcano, last erupted in 1917 and 1926
38.	**Trunyan:**	– *Bali Aga* (Original Balinese) village
39.	**Penelokan:**	– The place to look onto holy Mt. Batur and Lake Batur
40.	**Bangli:**	– Ancient capital, ca. 1204 A.D., with sacred temple Pura Kehen

KLUNGKUNG

41.	**Klungkung:**	– Noblest Balinese kingdom, last to succumb to Dutch, 1908
42.	**Gelgel:**	– Ancient capital city of the Kingdom of Klungkung
43.	**Kusamba:**	– Fishing and salt-making village; transit point to Nusa Penida
44.	**Nusa Penida:**	– Once a penal island for undesirables evicted from the Kingdom of Klungkung

KARANGASEM

45.	**Padangbai:**	– Landing point for cruise ships; old Muslim port of trade and transit to Lombok
46.	**Candidasa:**	– A new tourist beach-camp on white sands crescent
47.	**Tenganan:**	– Ancient *Bali Aga* (Original Balinese) village
48.	**Tirtaganggaa:**	– Magnificent rice fields and a modern water palace built in 1947
49.	**Amlapura:** (Karangasem)	– Site of powerful 18th century kingdom and eclectic palace, Bale London
50.	**Besakih:**	– Bali's holy *mother temple* complex, at 900m elevation
51.	**Gunung Agung:**	– The highest, holiest volcano, Bali's *Navel of the world*, last erupted in 1963

HISTORICAL CHRONOLOGY

6th century — A traveling Chinese Buddhist monk describes the island of "Po'li," believed to be Bali, as composed of some 136 villages set amid luxurious vegetation and ruled by a king believed to be a descendant of Hindu deities.

882 — The oldest dated inscription in Bali records the first king ruling Bali as Ugrasena, founder of the island's ancient and feudal Warmadewa Dynasty.

Late 10th century — The island of Bali is conquered by the Javanese king Dharmawangsa (989 -1007). His sister, Princess Mahendradatta, marries the Balinese king, Udayana.

1001 — Prince Erlangga is born. Son of the king Udayana and princess Mahendradatta, Erlangga returns to Java where he builds a powerful kingdom, rules Bali as part of his empire and lays the foundations of Javanese-Balinese political and cultural contact.

Early 12th century — Bali becomes a vassal of the eastern Javanese kingdom of Kediri.

1284 — The neighboring Javanese ruler, Kertanegara, re-conquers, pacifies and unifies Bali under the Singasari Dynasty.

1343 — Gajah Mada, Supreme General and Prime Minister of the Majapahit Empire, conquers Bali and introduces the Majapahit culture and its institutions. The Balinese are most receptive and the aristocracy eagerly seek to join their family trees to the ruling "Wong Majapahit".

1450 — The Hinduization of Bali proceeds through waves of migration and cultural infusion from the Majapahit Empire in the eastern part of Java.

1515 — The collapse of the Majapahit Empire (with the unstoppable rise of Islam) triggers a massive cultural migration to Bali. The last prince of Majapahit and his royal court of Hindu priests, artists, scholars, nobles and soldiers flee to Bali, transferring their culture intact.

1550 — Batu Renggong of the Gelgel Dynasty inherits the title of Dewa Agung, Great Deity or King, and initiates a political, military and cultural renaissance sometimes called Bali's "Golden Age." He controls all the Balinese rajahdoms and conquers Sumbawa and Lombok. Several generations later the family dynasty moves its court to Klungkung, which remains the "noblest" of the eight rajahdoms or principalities. (These rajahdoms are: Klungkung, Badung, Tabanan, Bangli, Gianyar, Karangasem, Buleleng and Jembrana).

1597 — The earliest Dutch trader, Cornelis de Houtman, arrives in Bali, searching for spices. Four members of the expedition are royally entertained by the court of Gelgel. Two men jump ship for the pleasures of tropical Bali, and the Western world receives fascinating reports about the island.

1601 — A Dutch expedition, led by Jacob van Heemskerck, tries to open trade with the island. The Dewa Agung presents him with a beautiful Balinese girl slave; and the Dutch interpret this as bestowing special rights upon them.

1639 — Di Made Bekung, last Dewa Agung of the "Golden Age" of the Gelgel Dynasty, provokes an invasion of Bali by the Javanese Empire of Mataram. He loses Sumbawa and Lombok and the allegiance of the other Balinese princes. The Gelgel court moves to Klungkung. They continue to symbolize Hindu imperial grandeur, but never again have real imperial power.

1667 — The rajahdom of Gianyar is born with the rise of Dewa Manggis Kuning, a fourth generation Gelgel. After early misadventures in Badung, Dewa Manggis escapes arrest — by being carried out of the palace wrapped in a woven mat carried atop an old servant's head. The fugitive prince sets up a Gianyar court which becomes a prosperous and powerful southern state.

1711 — The Dewa Agung's military and political power passes to Buleleng in the north. The joint rajahdom of Buleleng-Mengwi flourishes for the better part of the 18th century.

1717–1718 — Frequent hostilities between Bali and the Javanese Empire of Mataram climax in the destruction of East Java and Madura by roaming troops of Balinese. The Dutch refrain from real intervention in the Balinese-Javanese wars.

1740 — The rajahdom of Karangasem rises to prominence when it conquers Lombok. Rajah Gusti Gede Karangasem, a famous figure in Balinese history, subdues Buleleng, then Negara as well, dominating the political scene and stirring the populace to widespread resentment and anger.

1815 — Tambora Volcano on Sumbawa erupts. Buleleng and Singaraja, the large towns of north Bali, are damaged by ash and tidal waves. This is taken as a premonition of disaster.

1817 — The Dutch begin agricultural trade with Bali. Singaraja and Kuta become busy ports.

1826 — A permanent Dutch agent settles in Kuta, South Bali, beginning modern Dutch presence on the island. Captain J.S. Wetters' purpose is to recruit 1000 Balinese soldiers for the Dutch colonial army. The trade in opium and Balinese slaves flourishes under his influence.

1830s — Dutch traders begin to negotiate trade policies and sovereignty. The Balinese hold to a traditional concept of reef rights whereby villagers are entitled to plunder any ship that comes to grief near the island, accepting it as a gift of the gods.

1841 — The Dutch frigate *Overijsset* is wrecked on the Kuta reef and plundered of its cargo by Balinese. Amid furor and protest, a new Dutch commissioner lands at Buleleng. He is defied by a dramatic, dynamic young prince, Gusti Ketut Jelantik, the great hero of mid-19th century Bali.

1846 — Dutch-Bali wars. The first Dutch punitive expedition brings an invasion fleet of 58 vessels and 3000 well-armed men to defeat Jelantik's defense force in Buleleng. Danish trader Mads Lange, who runs a successful shipping and trading post in Kuta, acts as an intermediary and tries to negotiate a truce between the rajahs and the Dutch.

1848 — In the second Dutch punitive expedition the brilliant military leader Gusti Jelantik fights off three attacks with 25 cannon and 16,000 men.

1849 — The third and final Dutch expedition arrives with 100 armed vessels. The Dutch attack the Balinese stronghold at Jagaraga. The Balinese lose thousands, then advance in *puputan* (ritual suicide). The Dutch gains allies and troops from Lombok, who overtake the rajahs of Karangasem and Buleleng. The Balinese resistance is in complete disarray whilst the Dutch get stronger.

1850s — The Dutch "protective" administration assumes sovereign power over northern and western Bali. A new coffee plantation turns the north into a profitable colonial enterprise. Dutch ban the Hindu practice of *suttee*, the burning of widowed wives with their husbands, and take the first enlightened steps to wipe out slavery.

1868 — As the climax to the intermittent Gianyar-Klungkung wars, the rajahdom of Gianyar, the most prosperous and powerful state of the south, shatters the army of Klungkung.

1882 — Buleleng and Jembrana states are brought under direct Dutch rule. All Balinese women in that part of the island are ordered to cover their breasts.

1885 — The Dewa Manggis and his Gianyar retinue travel to Klungkung to pay homage to the Dewa Agung, but they are imprisoned instead and their ranks are destroyed. A rebellion of Muslim Sasaks in Lombok, vassals of the Balinese rulers of Karangasem, East Bali, is suppressed with cruelty.

1894 — The Dutch send a military expedition to Lombok to punish the Balinese rulers, but they are ambushed and massacred in the notorious "Lombok Treachery," at their camp in Cakranegara. To revenge their defeat, the Dutch lay to waste Lombok Island and raze Mataram to the ground in the process. The Balinese nobles perish in the mass rite of *puputan*, or ritual suicide, rather than surrender to the invaders. Dutch-Balinese relations are increasingly strained.

1900 — The Dutch annex Gianyar.

1904 — The Chinese schooner of *Sri Kumala* is wrecked near Sanur beach and is plundered. The Dutch demand compensation from the rajah of Badung, who remains defiant — and is backed up by the rajahs of Klungkung and Tabanan. The last *suttee* takes place in Tabanan this year.

1906 — A large Dutch military expedition lands at Sanur beach and troops march towards the royal palace in Denpasar. They are met by the rajah and his entire court, splendidly dressed for the tragic rite of *puputan*. In a ghastly suicide ceremony, the company turn their daggers and kris upon one another. The women tauntingly throw jewels at the Dutch soldiers. The entire court dies together and the battlefield before the burning palace is covered with mounds of corpses. The *puputan* ritual is repeated that same afternoon in Pemecutan, a minor court of Badung; and two days later in the court of the rajah of Tabanan.

1908 — Disorder and bombardment around Gelgel and Klungkung lead to the final *puputan* of the Dewa Agung and his court in Klungkung, the victims of

relentless western intrusion. The Dutch resolve to make amends. They introduce reforms under the Ethical Policy. They do not allow the presence of a Dutch colony, nor agricultural business, as in Java. Balinese farmers are protected against large-scale western exploitation and against the sudden impact of outside influences. A "conservationist" stance towards Balinese culture is taken and Dutch scholars usher in an era of achievements in art and architecture.

1920s—1930s — Foreign scholars, artists and musicians "discover" Bali. They record it and broadcast it to the world. Among the visitors are anthropologists Margaret Mead, Jane Belo and Gregory Bateson; artists Miguel Covarrubias. Walter Spies, Rudolf Bonnet, Arie Smit, Han Snel; musician Colin McPhee; writer Vicki Baum; and dancers and ethnologists Ted and Katharane Mershon.

1942 — Japanese Occupation. Japanese troops land at Sanur beach and control the island for three years, through headquarters at Denpasar and Singaraja. Walter Spies, Bali's most famous Western artist, perishes when a Japanese submarine torpedoes the ship on which he is being transported to safety as a German internee.

1945 — General Sukarno, a soldier and politician who has risen fast through the party ranks in Jakarta, declares *Merdeka* — Independence — for all the Indonesian archipelago. Dutch troops drive the Japanese out of Bali and try to reimpose a Dutch civil administration.

1946 — The battle for independence on Bali climaxes with the Margarana Incident in Tabanan state. A charismatic young Balinese military officer, Ngurah Rai — who relies not on tactics and logistics but upon intuition and mystical guidance — leads a suicide attack against Dutch forces and is martyred at Marga along with 95 followers.

1949 — The Hague concedes Indonesian independence. Bali becomes part of the Republic of the United States of Indonesia with Sukarno as its President.

1956 — Sukarno, President of Indonesia and "patron" of Bali island, builds various monuments such as the opulent Tampaksiring Palace, the bunker-like Bali Beach Hotel, and Udayana University which is now Bali's chief center of higher education.

1962 — A plague of rats infests Bali's fields and granaries. This is interpreted

as a divine signal of the displeasure and wrath of the dieties.

1963 — Gunung Agung, the holiest mountain, revered as the "Navel of the World," suddenly erupts without warning, killing over a thousand people and laying much of the island to waste. This volcanic catastrophe occurs while the Balinese are busy celebrating Eka Dasa Rudra, the most sacred of festivals, held only once every Balinese century at Pura Besakih, the mother temple on the slopes of Gunung Agung. The eruption is read as an evil omen.

1965 — Gestapu, the September 30 incident in Jakarta, is an abortive coup d'état; five top army generals are brutally mutilated by a clique of communist conspirators. Popular revulsion and desire for vengeance promotes a national blood-letting. In Bali thousands of suspected communists are killed in a matter of weeks.

1970s — Tourism develops in south Bali, in the capital city of Denpasar and in the beach resort villages of Sanur and Kuta. The Ngurah Rai International Airport in Tuban is opened. The government declares tourism the new industry and launches the development of the Nusa Dua mega-resort in the Bukit Peninsula.

1979 — On January 31st, in what in recent years has been called "the last great cremation," the remains of the Tjokorda Gde Agung Sukawati, the High Prince and would-have-been Rajah of Ubud, were burned in a huge black and gold bull sarcophagus.

1979 — Balinese island-wide again celebrate Eka Dasa Rudra on Mount Agung. Exactly 11 years and 11 days after the aborted festival of 1963, this massive celebration — involving the most elaborate preparations and animal sacrifices ever — is pronounced a success; the successful purging of the old and the blessed beginning of a new century of hope to the Balinese people.

1986 — American President Ronald Reagan, his wife, Nancy, and a host of other U.S. diplomats arrived here on April 29th to meet with Indonesia's President Suharto and the foreign ministers of the six Asean countries. As the Reagan entourage stepped off Air Force One at Ngurah Rai Airport, they were garlanded with flowers and greeted by President Suharto and a troupe of Balinese dancers. The U.S. President was on the island for four days.

DISCOGRAPHY-CASSETOGRAPHY
Compiled by Andy Toth

In 1928 the first records of music in Bali were made by the Odeon and Beka companies from Europe. Oddly enough, they were intended to be sold mainly in Indonesia, but the lack of any real market closed down the business and turned these 78s into collectors' items. In his book *A House in Bali* the composer-musicologist Colin McPhee describes how the dusty stacks of records in one shop were all smashed into oblivion by the frustrated shopkeeper. Percussive *gamelan* music produced fairly good recordings even with simple equipment, however, and these early recorded performances included the best orchestras and famous musicians. Tape copies of these old disks have inspired revivals of compositions long forgotten, and some are kept in ancestral shrines by families who for the first time would have heard their great-grandfathers' singing.

The following list of postwar LP records includes releases from the United States, Europe, and Japan. The first ones were made of the *gong kebyar* of Peliatan during their 1952 tour of Europe and America. The greatest interest and the largest number of recordings took place during studio sessions in the 1960s-70s.

Though foreign recording activity has died down, the local cassette industry in Bali has been booming since its start in 1970 along with tourism. Cassettes are copied in real time, and the typical company duplicating room is a sight to behold — banks of manually operated decks in a jungle of homegrown electronics and cables. Cassettes have not replaced live groups at ceremonies because Balinese music is group music-making, and much too active and important in such contexts. But tapes have proved convenient for dancers. Dancers can now buy a cassette with several takes of a single piece, so that practicing without a live group is no longer "rehearse and rewind." The mass media aspects of tape have also influenced the music scene, making Balinese more aware of regional styles, "new creations," and the dominance of the National Academy of Indonesian Dance in Denpasar (ASTI).

This list of cassettes is by no means extensive; one company alone has almost seven hundred recordings.

None of the vocal music or theater with dialogue has been included except for the popular Balinese dance and drama form called *sendratari*.

Asterisks* indicate records and cassettes that are particularly good in content or sound fidelity. For further details see *Recordings of the Traditional Music of Bali and Lombok*, Ann Arbor MI: Society for Ethnomusicology, 1980 (ISSN 0270-1766).

Balinese Cassette Companies
The first three of the following recording companies have good retail distribution, good sound fidelity and the widest selection. These are Bali Stereo, Aneka, and Nakula (followed by) Adiswara, Dewata, Indrawan and Rama. Tapes with superior sound quality however can be specially ordered from these recording studios.

Recordings of Western Performers
The Music of Bali (Colin McPhee and Benjamin Britten, piano), Schirmer Set No. 17 (513-515), 1941.
The Exotic Sounds of Bali (Univ. of Calif., Los Angeles), Columbia MS 6445 (ML 5845), 1963.
The Exotic Sounds of Bali (Univ. of Calif., Los Angeles), Columbia Odyssey 32-16-0366, 1966.
Tabuh-Tabuh Bali, Vol. 4 (Univ. of Calif., Los Angeles), Bali Stereo Cassette 173, 1974.
Kreasi Baru Gong Sekar Java (Oakland Calif.), Bali Stereo Cassette 580, 1978.

Records
The World of Gong Kebyar Dharma Santi, Victor (Japan) Digital SGS-31, 1982.
Music of Bali: Gamelan Gender Wayang, Lyrichord LLST 7360, 1982.
Bali: Gamelan Music from Sebatu Archive 2723-014, 1972.
Bali: Gamelan Music from Sebatu Archive 2533-130, 1972.
Music of Bali, Argo R6I 1952.
Music of Bali, Argo ARS 1006-1007, 1952.
Music from Bali, Argo ZFB 73, 1971.
Bali: Les Celebres Gamelans, Arion 30-U-103, 1972.
Les Orchestres de Gamelan de Bali, Barclay 920.383, 1971.
Panji in Bali I: Gamelan Semar Pengulingan, Barenreiter-Musicaphon BM 30 SL 2565, 1978.

Musique des Dieux, Musique des Hommes: Gamelans de Bali, Boite a Musique LD 096M, 1964.
Musique des Dieux, Musique des Hommes: Gamelans de Bali, Boite a Musique LD 5096, 1976.
Bali: Paradis des Iles de la Sonde, Boite a Musique Alvares LD 113, 1971.
Musique de Bali, Boite a Musique LD 339, 1952.
Bali: Musique Sacree, CBS France 65173, 1972.
Le Gamelan Balinais de Lotring, CBS France 88059, 1974.
Dancers of Bali, Columbia ML 4618, 1952.
Dancers of Bali, Columbia CMI 4618, 1972.
Dancers of Bali, Columbia AML 4618, 1974.
Bali, Centerpoint MC 20.113, 1953.
Gamelans de Bali, Denon XM-12-AM, 1966.
Bali: Folk Music, EMI-Odeon CO64-17858, 1972.
Musik aus Bali, EMi-Odeon 187-29645/6, 1976.
Bali: Le Gong Kebyar, Galloway GB 600528B, 1974.
Bali: Barong et Gender Wayang, Galloway GB 600529B, 1974.
Bali: Musiques de Danses, Vol. 1, Galloway GB 600534B, 1974.
Bali: Musiques de Danses, Vol. 2, Galloway GB 600535B, 1974.
Bali: Lelambatan, Galloway GB 600536B, 1974.
Bali: Le Culte des Morts, Galloway GB 600539B, 1974.
Golden Gong of Bali: Semar Pegulingan Grevillea GRV 1020, 1977.
Bali South, IE IER 7503, 1974.
Gamelan Music of Bali, Lyrichord LLST 7179 (LL 179), 1967.
Scintillating Sounds of Bali, Lyrichord LLST 7305, 1976.
Bali: The Celebrated Gamelans, Musical Heritage Society MHS 3505Z, 1977.
Bali-Java, Musidisc 30 CV 1110, 1966.
Music From the Morning of the World, Nonesuch H-72015 (H-2015), 1967.
Golden Rain, Nonesuch H-72028, 1968.
Music for the Balinese Shadowplay, Nonesuch H-72037, 1970.
Gamelan of the Love God: Gamelan Semar Pegulingan, Nonesuch H-72046, 1972.
Bali: Musique et Theater, Ocora OCR 60, 1972.

Bali: Divertissements Musicaux et Danses de Transe, Ocora OCR 72, 1973.
***Bali: Joged Bumbung,** Ocora 558-501, 1976.
***Bali: Le Gong Gede de Batur,** Ocora 558-510, 1976.
Musique de Bali, Pacific 1345-A-Std-1/2, 1968.
Music of Bali, SPL 1613.
The Gamelan Music of Bali, Peters International FARN 91009, 1976.
The Music From Bali, Philips 831-210 PL (631-210 PL), 1968.
***Bali: Court Music and Banjar Music,** Philips 6586-008, 1971.
***Balinese Theater and Dance Music,** Philips 6586-013, 1971.
Tabu-Tabuhan Bali: Music From Bali, Request SRLP 10101 (RLP 10101).
Music From Bali, United Artists UNS 15535 (UN 14535), 1967.
***Barong: Drame Musical Balinais,** Vogue LD 763, 1971.
Bali, Vogue MC 20.113.
Music of Bali, Westminster WAF 201.
Music of Bali, Westminster XWN 2209.
Bali: Matin du Monde, Boite a Musique LD 5787, 1972.
Gamelan de Bali, Barclay/Riviera Japan GT-5001, 1973.

Bali 1, Butterfly BLP 1007, 1973.
Bali 2, Butterfly BLP 1008, 1973.
Bali 3, Butterfly BLP 1009, 1973.
Kecak Peliatan of Bali, Seven Seas GXC-5001, 1978.
The Barong Dance of Bali, Seven Seas GXC-5015, 1978.
Musique Traditionelle de Bali, Vogue Loisirs CLVLXEK 264.
***Music of the Orient (old Odeon recordings),** Decca USA DX 107, 1951.

Cassettes
***Kreasi Baru ASTI, Vol. 1,** Bali Stereo 600.
***Tari Lepas dan Kreasi Baru ASTI, Vol. 2,** Bali Stereo 601.
Sendratari Mahabharata Abimanyu Antaka ASTI, Bali Stereo 603.
***Kreasi Baru Antologi Karawitan Bali,** Bali Stereo 604.
***Lelambatan dan Koor,** Bali Stereo 609.
***Pelegongan Klasik,** Bali Stereo 610.
Sendratari Mahabharata Gugurnya Senapati Salya, Bali Stereo 616.
Sendratari Mahabharata Mosala Parwa, Bali Stereo 617.
***Tari Belibis ASTI,** Bali Stereo 624.
Tari Kreasi Baru Ujian Sarjana Muda 1985 ASTI, Bali Stereo 625-628.

Sendratari Mahabharata Narakesuma ASTI, Bali Stereo 630.
Sendratari Ramayana Uttara Kanda ASTI, Bali Stereo 632.
***Kreasi Gong Kebyar ASTI,** Bali Stereo 636.
***Gong Lelambatan Gladag Badung,** Bali Stereo 639.
***Kreasi Baru Ujian Tingkat Seniman 1985 ASTI — Kindama,** Bali Stereo 640.
***Gamelan Gender Kayumas Kaja Badung,** Bali Stereo 643-644.
***Angklung Semara Mekar Abian Semal,** Bali Stereo 647-649.
***Tari Lepas Kreasi Baru ASTI, Vol. 1 — Manuk Rawa,** Aneka 546.
***Kreasi Gong Kebyar ASTI, Vol. 4,** Aneka 551.
Angklung Lelambatan Kayumas Kelod, Aneka 541.
***Tabuh Klasik Semar Pegulingan Binoh Badung,** Aneka 470-471.
***Tari Lepas ASTI, Vol. 2,** Aneka 547.
Sendratari Mahabharata Matinya Kicaka, Aneka 550.
***Jegog Mendoyo,** Aneka 364.

Gong Agung Sekar Sandat Sulahan Bangli, Bali Stereo 421.
***Joged Bumbung Semara Yasa Bukit Jangkrik Gianyar,** Nakula 05.
Gong Beleganjur Batugaing Beraban, Nakula 16.
***Gong Pindha,** Aneka 09.
Kreasi Festival se-Bali, Aneka 59.
Kreasi Festival Gong, Aneka 68.
***Gong Surya Kencana Pangkung Tabanan,** Aneka 79-81.
***Kreasi dan Lelambatan Gong Pinda,** Aneka 216.
***Gong Br. Anyar Perean,** Aneka 236-237, 239.
***Gong Jaya Kesuma Gladag Badung,** Aneka 269-270.

Compact Discs
Fantastic and Meditatine Gamelan/ 'Tirta Sasi' — Samas Pegulingam of Peliatan Village in Bali, Victor (Japan) VDP-1103, Compact Disc, from analog master.
***Gamelan Music in Bali,** CBS/Song (Japan) 32 DG 58, Compact Disc, from digital master, ASTI Banpasar group.
Bali: Musiques De l'Asia traditionelles, Vol. 3, Playa Sound PS 33503.
Musik aus Bali, EMI — Electrola 187-29-645/646.

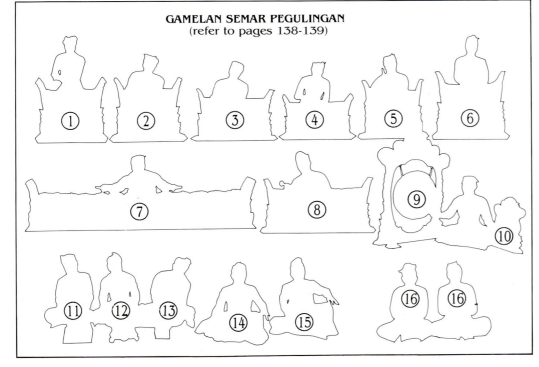

GAMELAN SEMAR PEGULINGAN
(refer to pages 138-139)

① Gangsa Jegogan ② Gangsa Calung ③ Gangsa Permade
④ Gangsa Kantilan ⑤ Gangsa Calung ⑥ Gangsa Jegogan
⑦ Trompong ⑧ Gender Rambat ⑨ Gong ⑩ Klentong ⑪ Kajar
⑫ Ceng-ceng (or Rincik) ⑬ Kienang ⑭ Kendang Lanang (male drum) ⑮ Kendang Wadon (female drum) ⑯ Suling (flute)
Not pictured: Gentorag (bell tree) and Rebab (bowed spike lute)

BALI FILMOGRAPHY
Compiled by John A.C. Darling

Bali has inspired moviemakers in much the same way it has still photographers, though sometimes with mixed results. Indeed, any film-maker faced with surviving a winter in less tropical climes more than welcomes a chance to shoot footage in the tropics. And in Bali, despite some of the technical difficulties involved, one knows that he will both have a good time and come back with memorable and beautiful motion picture sequences. Since the 1920s, Bali has attracted scores of such film-makers, all of them keen to capture the vibrancy of color and ritual that are standard fare on the island. The result has been both good and bad films. The good films have become important documentary classics, but the bad ones — and there are many — have faded into celluloid obscurity.

The following selected filmography includes upward of 100 Bali-related films, some of them very good, but most of them interesting only as cinematic footnotes. The list is not exhaustive, so the publishers of this book would like to invite readers to forward us any additional information or entries that can be added to the list in future editions of this book.

1926
Bali-Leichenverbrennung und Einascherung einer Furstenwitwe. (16½ min).
Bali-Sanghijang und Ketjaqtanz. (5 min). Holland. Both the above two films were made by W. Mullens. This first film about a cremation in Bali is quite remarkable.

1929
Mahasoetji: Van Java's Vulkanengweld en het Wondere Bali. Holland, 35mm, B & W, 16 frames per second, 5 reels, (total length: 2271 meters). 1.0. Ochse. Produktie: NIFM, Haariem/Buittenzorg.

193?
Bali. USA, B & W silent, (8 min)., (Library of Congress, Washington).

1931
The Island of Demons, (Die Insel des Daemonen). Germany. Producer-Director, Victor Baron von Plessen; Camera, Dr. Dalsheim; Scenario, casting and choreography, Walter Spies. This is still the classic film about Bali. It tells a fictional story of young lovers thwarted by greed and black magic in a 100 per cent correct ethnographic background.

The photography is absolutely stunning both in framing and in the use of light and shadow. The story line is strong and very understandable both in a Western and Balinese context. It was for this film that Walter Spies remodelled the *Kecak*, the so-called "monkey dance," into the form that till this day enthralls and amazes visting tourists. Spies' only complaint with the completed film after he traveled to Surabaya to see it was with the musical score, which is typical 1930s movie music. Spies' criticism and disappointment is understandable as he had specially re-scored original *gamelan* composition for two pianos to be used in this important film.

1932
Goona Goona, An Authentic Melodrama. (Also called, *Der Kris, The Kris,* 1931, in Europe). USA, 35mm, B & W, by Andre Roosevelt and Armand Denis. Shot in Bali in 1928-29. In 1930s Hollywood the topless look was called "goona goona", such was the impact of this film and the delight of the film producers in the beautiful women of Bali. This film features the famous I Mario, creator of the *Kebyar* dance.

1935
Tropisch Nederlands. Holland, B & W, optical sound. Originally in three parts entitled: "Maha Suci", "Maha Kuasa" and "Maha Sila". A very fine film. A re-issue of the earlier 1929 version.

1936
Lelong: a film of Bali, shown in color. By the Marquis de la Falaise de la Coudraye. Believed to be the first film on Bali made in color. A review in the anthropological journal *Man*, vol. 36, 1936, pp 96-7 describes it as "an aesthetic production of great beauty which has already received recognition in an international exhibition in Moscow. Though made primarily for commercial purposes it embodies many details of general anthropological interest, giving a record, in particular, of bethrothal customs, traditional dances and mortuary rites. The script was discussed in detail and approved by the elders of the village where the film was mainly taken, and in his commentary the Marquis de la Falaise pointed out precisely where and for what reasons it departed from Balinese custom. This and his account of the difficulties of film production in a native community throw interesting sidelights on the contact of

cultures." We would be greatful for any information about where a copy of this film might now be held.

1937
Tanze auf Bali. Zurich, Switzerland. Made by C.A Schlaepfer. (6 min).

1938
An East Indian Island. USA, B & W, silent, (11 min), Andre de la Varre.
Speertanze, Reiniguns-Zerimonien und Totenfeirlicchkeiten auf Bali. (11½ min).
Barong-Keket-Tanz auf Bali. (21 min).
Tanzunterricht, Kebyar-aud Legong-Tanz auf Bali. (11½ min).
Baris-Djauk-Tanz auf Bali. (11½ min).
Ketjak, Kinder-Barong und Kinder-Djanger auf Bali. (10 min).
The above five films were all made by the German adventurer and film-maker Victor Baron von Plessen, who also made the superb feature film *The Island of Demons* (see under Year 1931.)
Reishau auf Bali. Germany, H. Nevermann.
Impian Bali. Indonesia (Dutch East Indies). Produced by Tan's Film. Further information about this film would be most welcome.

1939
Bali, (44 min, 16mm, color, silent at sound speed, with captions) USA. Michael Lerner. A portrayal of life on the island of Bali.
Bali, The Lost Paradise. (12 min, B & W, 16mm, silent). USA, Michael Lerner.

1940
Dance of the Eyes. A film by Mel Nichols for Shell, Australia. An interesting short 16mm, B & W film on dancing in Bali.

1941
Noesa Penida. Indonesia, The New Java Industrial Film Company. Directed by Andjar Asmara. Believed to be one of the first films directed by a "pribumi" Indonesian.

1947
In the Shadow of the Waringen-Bali. Holland, N. Multifilm. 16 mm, B & W, optical sound. Dutch Government propaganda film.
De Dans. (Dances of Indonesia). Holland, 16mm, B & W, optical sound, (20 min).

1948
Indonesia Calling. Australia, B & W, (22 min). Political film (by Joris Ivens) produced by the Australian Waterside Workers' Federation to express their identification with and support for the

independence movement in Indonesia against Dutch colonialism.

1949

Bali I Farver og Fest. Copenhagen, Denmark, by A.K. Nielsen, (54 min). *Bali in Bild und Wort, Besuch beim Fursten von Ubud.*

1951

Bali Today. USA, 16mm, color, sound. (10 min), (Encyclopedia Britannica).

1952

Road to Bali. USA, Paramount, Technicolor (91 min). Bob Hope, Dorothy Lamour, Bing Crosby and the Peliatan dance group led by the venerable Anak Agung Mandera. Shot in Hollywood. The color makes the sets all too obvious. Not the best of the "The Road" series of travel films.

Trance and Dance in Bali. USA, by Gregory Bateson and Margaret Mead, B & W, (22 min). A famous film about the *Calonarang* dance and ritual which shows some extraordinary scenes of trance. (New York University Film Library).

Childhood Rivalry in Bali and New Guinea. USA, N.Y.U., B & W, (20 min). How mothers in two differing societies handle sibling rivalry. The material for this film was shot by Gregory Bateson and Margaret Mead during the 1930s.

A Balinese Family. USA, (16 min), Bateson and Mead. N.Y.U.

Bathing Babies in Three Cultures. USA, (9 min), Bateson and Mead. N.Y.U.

1954

Si Melati. Indonesia, 16mm, B & W, Bazuki Effendi. Feature film, well photographed but otherwise fairly basic.

1955

Djayaprana. Indonesia, 16mm, B & W, Perusahaan Film Negara (State Film Company) Kotot Sukardi. The original classic of the North Bali legend of love, lust and magic; a tragedy. In the early 1950s a cult developed around the legend of Jayaprana and Layonsari.

Sukreni Gadis Bali. Indonesia, Bali Films Ltd. Based on the novel by the prolific Balinese author, A.A. Pandji Tisna.

1956

East is East. USA, 35mm, 2 reels, color, sound, (Warner Bros). Believed to have a small section on Bali.

196?

Midday Sun and Night. By David Attenborough for the BBC. Two one-hour films about the dance and culture of Bali with John Coast.

1962

Holiday in Bali. Indonesia/Philippines joint production. Djamaudin Malik, Misbach Yuser Biran and Tony Ceyado.

1969

Indonesia — The Substance and the Shadow. Australia, John Cockcroft, Career Productions and Mutual Life and Citizens' Assurance, color, (55 min). Life, culture and industry of Indonesia, filmed in Java, Bali and Sumatra.

1970

Adventure in Bali. Indonesia, Usmar Ismail. Some mystery surrounds this film because Usmar, the great founder of the Indonesian film industry died during 1970.

Bali — Island of Gods and Demons.

Bali — Island of Magic.

Bali — Island of the Gods. Australia. All three by Talisman Productions and Mutual Life and Citizens' Assurance. Each film in color, 12 min. each.

197?

Bali Today. USA, Hartley Productions, 16mm, color, (18 min). The famous anthropologist Dr. Margaret Mead visits Bali and shares her insights into Balinese society.

1972

Perawan Bali (Virgin in Bali). Indonesia, Dharmaputra Film Djaya, Producer: Brigadier-General Sofjar. Co-production with Italian-Swiss production Company. Starring: Enny Soekamto. A feature film that had great success and popularity throughout Indonesia.

Morning of the Earth. Australia, Alby Falzon. Surfing on lovely Bali.

Tamu. Australia, Ian Stocks and Jane Oehr, 16mm, color, (54 min). A film about the well-known Australian artist, writer, and raconteur Donald Friend who lived on the island of Bali during the 1960s and 1970s. The film describes Balinese culture and shows the artist at work on the island.

Kabut di Kintamani (Clouds Over Kintamani). Indonesia, P.T. Avadara Film. 35mm, color. By Kurnaen Suhardiman. Well-regarded social realism.

1973

Bali: Religion in Paradise. USA, 16mm, color, (30 min), Directions, Eastern Religions Series, American Broadcasting Companies Inc.

Bali, Island of the Gods. Japan, 16mm, color, (60 min plus), Jun'ichi Ushiyama.

A film on the culture of Bali by the famous ethnographic film-maker.

Island of the Spirits. Australia, Cinetel Productions, Frank and Josette Heimans. 16mm., color, (50 min). The cremation of Cokorda Sudharsana of Ubud. (Also available in French).

1974

Tabuh Tabuhan. Australia, ABC-TV. 16mm, color, (50 min). The Australian composer Peter Sculthorpe explores Balinese *gamelan* music.

1975

Emmanuelle 2. France, Trinarce Films, starring Sylvia Kristel and Umberto Orsini. Emmanuelle's erotic adventures in the Far East; love blossoms in Bali.

A Balinese Gong Orchestra. Film Australia, Sydney (*Our Asian Neighbors: Indonesia,* series). Video, 16mm, color, (11 min).

Mestri: A Balinese Woman. Film Australia, Sydney (*Our Asian Neighbors: Indonesia,* series) (18 min). Mastri is a dancer in a village dance group which sometimes performs at the tourist hotels.

Mask of Rangda. USA, 16mm, color, (30 min). Made for Garuda Indonesian Airways. A dramatic interpretation of the fearsome trances that accompany Calonarang dance performances.

Sacred Trances of Java and Bali. USA, 16mm, color, (30 min). Made for Garuda Indonesian Airways.

Alternative Lifestyles. Australia, Leigh Tilson. 16mm, color, (15 min). A witty film about cultural change in Bali.

1976

Twist in the Trail. Australia, ABC-TV. The overland hippy trail from Australia to Europe passes through Bali.

Asian Insight-Indonesia. Australia, John Temple and Arch Nicholson, co-production from ABC-TV and Film Australia. This episode from a six-part series on the nations of Asia has a section devoted to Bali.

Balas Dendam. Indonesia, H. Djohardin, Boby Sandi and Chun Chong Hua, P.T. Elang Perkasa Film. A co-production with Hong Kong. A kung-fu thriller set in Bali.

1977

In Search of Tubullar Swells. USA, Dick Hoole and Jack McCoy. Includes stunning footage of surfing at Uluwatu.

1978

Bali. A series of 23 short films on many differing aspects of Balinese culture, music, weaving, etc. made by Dr Urs

Ramseyer of the Basel Museum. (These films are available from the Basel Museum and the Institut Fur Den Wissenschaftlichen Film, Nonnstieg, 3400 Gottingen, West Germany).

Learning to Dance in Bali. USA, Gregory Bateson and Margaret Mead, produced by Beryl Bernay and Maher Benham. An interesting film put together from materials shot in Bali during the 1930s. Of particular interest is footage of the great dancer, I Mario, who invented the Kebyar dance.

Face Values. UK, BBC Education, David Cordingly. Six one-hour episodes studying comparitive behaviour in five cultures including Bali. With Royal anchor-man H.R.H. Prince Charles.

Jalur Bali. Indonesia, Sjundodo Ardibruto and Njonja Jean Mandagi.

Bali Connection. Indonesia, P.T. Imeda Films, Motinggo Boesje. Another smuggling story of which Bali is one of the locations.

1979

Balinese Surfer. UK, BBC-TV, The World About Us series, (53 min)., Bill Leimbach. A young balinese dancer learns to surf. (Available from Survival Films, 1065 Barrenjoey Road, Palm Beach, NSW. 2108, Australia).

Bali Vision. UK, BBC-TV, 16 mm, color, (30 min), (*Everyman* series), Bill Leimbach. Media guru Dr. Lawrence Blair shows his view of Bali.

The Cremation of a Balinese Prince. Holland, NOS-TV. The cremation of Cokorda Agung Sukawati, the king of Ubud, and of his great friend, the Dutch artist Rudolf Bonnet.

The Eleven Powers. Australia, Larry Gartenstein and Frank Heimans, 16mm, color, (54 min). Narration by Orson Welles. A film about Eka Desa Rudra, the great once-a-hundred-years ritual at Pura Besakih on the slopes of Gunung Agung. The Balinese undertake to purify the world. Winner of a Gold Award at the 1981 New York Film Festival.

Bali-Pulau Dewata. Australia, 16mm, color, (17 min). A film made for Qantas Airways by prominent Australian film-makers Phil Noyce and David Elfick.

Bali and Java. Australia, 16mm, color, (20 min). For Qantas as above.

1980

Lempad of Bali. Australia, by John Darling and Lorne Blair, 16mm, color, (56 min). A film about the life and death of the 116-year-old master artist. This film shows the elaborate cremation rites for I Gusti Nyoman Lempad, the development of his many artistic talents and the history of the island during his lifetime. "One of the (Asian) festival's highlights was the world premiere of a stunning documentary, Lempad of Bali...", *Hollywood Reporter*, 8 JULY 1980. Winner of the Mitra Award at the 20th Asian Film Festival. (Available from the Australian Film Commission, 8 West St, North Sydney, NSW, Australia). (Also available in Bahasa Indonesia).

A Balinese Trance Seance. Australia, by Linda Connor and Timothy Asch, 16mm, color, (30 min) A traditional healer mediates between the supernatural and human worlds. (Documentary Educational Resources, 5 Bridge Street, Watertown, Mass., 02172, USA).

1981

Bali High. Stephen Spaulding and Alexis Thomas. Surfing Adventure.

Tales of the Seven Seas. USA, Scott Dittrich. Good surf from Bali and around the world.

Schonheit Und Reichtum Des Lebens (Beauty and Riches). Holland, IKON-TV. 16mm, color, by Hans Hulscher. A documentary film about the life and times of the German artist Walter Spies who lived in Bali during the 1930s and who contributed significantly to the development of the Balinese modern art movement of that time

The Three Worlds of Bali. USA, 16mm, color, (58 min). (PBS-TV, Odyssey Series.) Ira Abrams and Steve Lansing. Describes the three realms of Bali: the mountains for the gods, the sea for the demons and the middle land for humankind. Also includes footage of Eka Dasa Rudra, the once-a-hundred-year rite. (Distributed by Documentary Educational Resources, 5 Bridge Street, Watertown, Mass., 02172, USA).

Margaret Mead: Taking Note. USA, 16mm, color, (58 min), (Odyssey Series, PBS-TV), Ann Peck. A review of Dr. Mead's life and work, includes some interesting footage of Bali.

Jero on Jero: A Balinese Trance Seance Observed. Australia, 16mm, color, (17 min). Linda Connor, Tim and Patsy Asch. A trance medium looks at herself on film in trance. (Documentary Educational Resources, 5 Bridge Street, Watertown, Mass., USA, 02172).

Mistik (Leyak). Indonesia, P.T. Pan Asiatic Films. Written by Putra Madé. Story of a western woman studying black magic on the island of Bali.

1982

The Spirit of Asia. UK, BBC-TV, David Attenborough and Michael Macintyre. This larger-than-life series has one episode devoted entirely to Bali. Other episodes also have materials on Bali, including those on the Eka Dasa Rudra ritual held once every 100 years.

The Human Race. UK, ITV. A series presented by Desmond Morris. The episode called "Art and Religion" includes a considerable essay about a Balinese temple festival.

The Medium is the Masseuse: A Balinese Massage. Australia, The Australian National University, 16mm, color, (35 min), Linda Connor, Tim and Patsy Asch. (Documentary Educational Resources, 5 Bridge Street, Watertown, Mass., USA, 02172).

The Forgotten Voyage. UK, BBC-TV, (73 min). Shot in actual locations, including Bali, this documentary drama features the epic research endeavors of the naturalist-biologist Alfred Russel Wallace, who at the same time as Charles Darwin formulated the theory of the "Origin of Species." He is also well-known for his classic book *The Malay Archipelago* (which chronicles his trip there) and for his observations which gave rise to the Wallace's Line (between Bali and Lombok) which divides the fauna of Asia from that of Australasia.

Bali-Down from the Mountain. UK, BBC-TV, (25 min). This program examines the social uses of water in Balinese culture. Some of the ideas of the different links between water and purity are explored. Includes a *Calonarang* performance. Filmed around the village of Djumpai in South-east Bali.

Bali-Cremation. UK, BBC-TV. A cremation ritual from the village of Kamasan.

1983

Bali. Germany, A tele-movie directed by the maker of *Mephisto*, Isvan Szabo. A film director making a documentary about the artist Walter Spies decides to throw over his western life-style and instead imitate the subject of his documentary film.

The Autobiography of a Balinese Healer. Australia, 16mm, color, Linda Connor, Tim and Patsy Asch. (Documentary Educational Resources, 5 Bridge Street, Watertown, Mass., USA, 02172).

Right: A series of Kamasan-style panel details show what will happen to you if you lead a sinful life and are committed to the Balinese hell in your afterlife. These nasty visions appear on the lower ceiling of the Kerta Gosa, or Hall of Justice, courtroom in Klungkung.

Shadow Master. USA, 16mm, color, (50 min) by Larry Reed. A young man learns to be a Balinese shadow-puppeteer in a fast-changing world.

Balinese Dancer. Indonesia, Dea Sudarman, 16mm, color, (20 min). A day in the life of a Balinese dancer.

Hungry to Paint. Indonesia, Pusat Perusahaan Film Negara, Yazir Marzuki, 16mm, color, (30 min). The famous Indonesian artist Affendi talks about his art and life. The film shows Affendi at work on location in Java and Bali and at home (in Yogyakarta) with his two wives.

Jayaprana. Indonesia, 35mm, color, Kardar Djona. Remake of the 1955 film about the legend of Bali.

1984

Saat Saat Yang Indah. Indonesia, 35mm, color, by Sufan Sufiran. A Jakarta man on business in Bali has an affair with a Balinese woman. Unaware he has left the woman pregnant, he returns to Jakarta, marries and has a family. Back in Bali the mother and child are rejected by their family. After the death of his mother the boy goes to Jakarta to search for his father. A well-made feature film.

1985

Master of the Shadows. Film Australia, directed by John Darling, from the five-part series "The Human Face of Indonesia." A *dalang* (priest-puppeteer) tells of his life and art and talks about some of the problems facing present-day Bali. (Available from the Australian Film Commission, 8 West Street, North Sydney, NSW, Australia).

The New Pacific. UK, BBC and R.M. Productions Munich. Michael Mcintyre. A series on the Far East, the Pacific and other developing countries of the Pacific basin. Includes material from Bali.

1986

Ngarap. Australia, The Australian National University, 16mm, color, (20 min), Anthony Forge and Patsy Asch. A study of fighting over the corpse and other violent and unusual behavior associated with some cremations in Bali. Shot on location in Bali during 1977.

Quest for Healing. Australia, Independent Productions, Richard Davis, shot in 1985. A series of six films about traditional and alternative healing around the world. This series contains some remarkable material on the healing practices of Bali.

Life Rituals of Bali & Bali — The Mountain to the Sea. Australia, John Darling. Two one-hour documentaries which were begun in 1982. With *Lempad of Bali* these films will be John Darling's film documentary record of the culture of the island of Bali.

Revolt in Paradise. Australia. McElroy & McElroy of *Picnic of Hanging Rock* and *The Year of Living Dangerously* are well advanced in their plans to film the adventures of a Manx woman in Bali during the 1930s, the turbulent years of the Japanese occupation and Indonesia's fight for independence against the Dutch.

Another perfunctory part of every packaged Bali travel itinerary is the spectacular barong dance. During dances such as this one being staged in a tourist temple at Batubulan, a leonine barong highsteps during a performance well worth the price of admission. *Real* barong dances, however, are a very serious affair.

BIBLIOGRAPHY

This bibliography gives but a fraction of the available literature on Bali, primarily the most popularly available, and in the judgement of the author, the most interesting for an eclectic, enlightened and generally English-reading audience.

Bali: Isle of Temples and Dances, Department of Information, Republic of Indonesia, Jakarta, (1960).

Bali: The Isle of Gods, Department of Information, Republic of Indonesia, Jakarta.

Bandem, I. Made and de Boer, Fredrick Eugene, *Kaja and Kelod: Balinese Dance in Transition,* Oxford University Press, Kuala Lumpur (1981).

Bateson, Gregory and Mead, Margaret, *Balinese Character: A Photographic Analysis,* New York Academy of Sciences, New York (1942).

Baum, Vicki, *A Tale from Bali,* Oxford University Press, Singapore (1973). (Original: G. Bles, London, 1937.)

Black, Star, *Guide to Bali,* Apa Productions, Singapore (1975).

Blackwood, Sir Robert, *Beautiful Bali,* Hampden Hall, Melbourne (1970).

Beath, Betty and Cox David, *Spice and Magic,* Boolarong Publications, Brisbane (1983).

Belo, Jane, *Bali: Rangda and Barong. Monographs of the American Ethnological Society, 16.* University of Washington Press, Seattle (1949).

Belo, Jane, *Trance in Bali,* Columbia University Press, New York (1960).

Belo, Jane, editor, *Traditional Balinese Culture,* Columbia University Press, New York : 1970).

Boon, J. A., *The Anthropological Romance of Bali 1597-1972: Dynamic perspectives in marriage and caste, politics and religion,* Cambridge University Press, Cambridge (1977).

Cartier-Bresson, Henri (photographs), *Les Danses a Bali,* Collection Huit, Paris (1954).

Covarrubias, Miguel, *Island of Bali,* Oxford University Press, Kuala Lumpur (1972). (Original by Knopf, New York 1938.)

Covernton, Mary and Wheeler, Tony, *Bali and Lombok: A Travel Survival Kit,* Lonely Planet, South Yarra, Australia (1983).

Cool, Captain William, *With the Dutch in the East: An Outline of the Military Operations in Lomboc, 1894,* The Java Head Bookshop, London (1934).

Eiseman, Fred, *Bali: Sekala and Niskala,* a collection of essays, Eiseman, Scottsdale, Arizona (1985).

Geertz, Clifford, *The Interpretation of Cultures,* Basic Books, New York (1973).

Geertz, Clifford, *The Theater State in Nineteenth Century Bali,* Princeton University Press, Princeton (1980).

Geertz, Hilda and Geertz, Clifford, *Kinship in Bali,* The University of Chicago Press, Chicago (1975).

Goris, R. and Dronkers, P.L., *Bali: Atlas kebudajaan, Cults and Customs, Cultuurgeschiedenis in beeld,* Ministry of Education and Culture of the Republic of Jakarta (1955).

Gralapp, Leland W., *Balinese Painting: The Taylor Museum Collection,* Taylor Museum of Colorado Springs Fine Arts Center, 1961.

Grant, Ian, *Bali, Morning of the World,* A.H. and A.W. Reed, Wellington (1970).

Hanna, Willard A., *Bali Profile: people, events, circumstances (1001-1976),* American Universities Field Staff, New York (1976).

Hilbery, Rosemary, *A Balinese Journal, 1971-1980,* Percetakan Dharma Bhakti, Denpasar (1980).

Hiss, Philip Hanson, *Bali,* Robert Hale, London, 1941.

Hogan, Rae, *Guide to Bali,* Paul Hamlyn, Sydney-London-New York-Toronto (1974).

Holt, Claire, *Art in Indonesia: Continuities and Change,* Cornell University Press, Ithaca (1967).

Hooykaas, C, *Cosmogony and Creation in Balinese Tradition,* M. Nijhoff, The Hague (1974).

Hooykaas, C, *Kama and Kala: Materials for the Study of Shadow Theater in Bali,* Northern Holland Publishing Company, Amsterdam (1973).

Hooykaas, C, *Religion in Bali,* E.J. Brill, Leiden (1973).

Hooykaas, C., *Tovenarij op Bali: Magische tekeningen,* Meulenhoff, Amsterdam (1980).

Kempers, *Monumental Bali: Introduction to Balinese Archaeology (A guide to the monuments),* Van Goor Zonen den Haag, Arhem, Holland (1977).

de Kleen, Tyra, *The Temple Dances in Bali,* Borfor Lager Gothia Aktiebolag, Stockholm (1952). (First edition, 1936.)

Krause, B., *Bali, Vol I: Land un Volk; Vol II: Tanze, Tempel, Feste,* Folkwang Verlag, Hagen (1920).

Mabbet, Hugh, *The Balinese,* January Books, New Zealand (1985).

Mason, Victor, *The Haughty Toad and Other Tales from Bali* (illustrated by artists of Pengosekan), Paul Hamlyn, Sydney and P.T. Bali Art Print, Sanur, Bali (1975).

Matthews, Anna, *The Night of Purnama,* Oxford University Press, Kuala Lumpur (1983). (Original publication, 1965.)

McPhee, Colin, *A House in Bali,* Oxford University Press, Singapore (1984). (Original publication, 1944.)

Mershon, Katharane E., *Seven Plus Seven: Mysterious Life Rituals in Bali,* Vantage Press, New York (1971).

Moerdowo, R, *Ceremonies in Bali,* Kanisius, Jogjakarta (1973).

Moore, Joanna, *Bali, Island of a Thousand Temples,* Donald Moore for Asia Pacific Press, Singapore (1970).

Mrazek, Rudolf and Bedrich Forman (photographs by Werner Forman), *Bali: The Split Gate to Heaven,* Orbis Publishing, London (1983).

de Panthou, Patrick (photographs by Leonard Lueras, Kal Muller), *Bali,* (Les Editions du Pacifique), Singapore (1978).

Powell, Hickman, *The Last Paradise,* Oxford University Press, Kuala Lumpur (1982). (Original publication, 1930)

Ramseyer, Urs, *Art and Culture of Bali,* , Oxford University Press, Oxford (1977).

Reyes, Elizabeth, *Bali,* Times Travel Library series, Times Editions, Singapore (1987).

Rhodius, Hans and Darling, John, *Walter Spies and Balinese Art,* Terra, Zutphen, Amsterdam (1980).

Rump, Peter, *Bali and Lombok,* Globetrotter, Bielefeld (1984).

Santosa, Silvio, *Gianyar: Valley of the Ancient Relics, Art and Culture,* Regency Government of Gianyar, Bali (1985).

Toth, Andrew (editor), *Recordings of Traditional Music of Bali and Lombok,* The Society for Ethnomusicology, Inc, Providence, Rhode Island (1980).

Uhlig, Helmut, *Insel del Lebenden Gotter,* C. Bertelsmann Verlag, Munchen (1979).

Wijaya Madé, *Balinese Architecture: Towards an Encyclopedia, Vol I & II,* Fotokopi Series, Denpasar (1985).

Wijaya Madé, *The Complete "Stranger in Paradise"* (a collection of *Bali Post* columns of 1979), House of Xerox, Jakarta (1984).

De Zoete, Beryl and Spies, Walter, *Dance and Drama in Bali,* Faber and Faber, London (1938).

INDEX

Following pages: A sunset-to-twilight time exposure of the Pura Ulundanu, an impressive lake spirits temple that rises like a sentinel above Lake Batur in the Kintamani area. This temple was rebuilt on higher ground by local villagers following its nearly total destruction in 1926 during a violent eruption of nearby Gunung Batur. Only the temple's sacred main shrine survived that debacle.

ACKNOWLEDGEMENTS

Before continuing on to other exotic books and places, the author and photographer would like to acknowledge and thank some of the people who made this book possible. We are first of all grateful to Didier Millet and Jane Perkins, Times Editions' managing director and chief editor respectively, who believed in this book and initially commissioned its creation; Chow Yeow Teck and Woon Mee Lan, who guided the book through its complex design and production stages; editors Tan Kok Eng, Stu Glauberman and Andy Toth, who proofread manuscripts; and Nedra Chung, who helped with preliminary research. Thanks also to Toth, John Darling and Liz Reyes for their work on appendices matters; Leo Haks and Michael Sweet for their help in locating rare archival photographs and prints; and Time-Life, Inc., (New York), the Ernst Haas Studio (New York), and the Magnum Photo Agency (Paris) for file photographs reproduced in this book.

On the island of Bali, numerous people contributed to this effort in many important ways. Chief among these were Suteja Neka of the Neka Museum, Campuan-Ubud; Verra Darwiko of the Arts of Asia antique shop, Denpasar; Wija and Agus Waworuntu of the Hotel Tandjung Sari, Sanur; I Madé Budi of Batuan; Rio Helmi of Ubud's Cafe Lotus; Brent Hesselyn, the island's senior ceramicist; and Jimmy Jaman of Bali Tours, Ltd. Other persons and institutions who offered timely aid and comfort were Dr. A. A. M. Djelantik, David Stuart-Fox, I Madé Djimat, Peter Jennings, Jessieca Leo, Charlie Kushner, Kristina Melcher, I Wayan Wija, Mary Zurbuchen, Koes, Michel Gelenine, Hans Rhodius (and the Walter Spies foundations of Bali and Holland), Bruce Carpenter (and the W. O. J. Nieuwenkamp family and foundation) and Peter and Madé Steenbergen of Madé's Warung, Kuta. Finally, we would like to say *terima kasih banyak* to our Balinese friends Wayan, Madé, Nyoman and K'tut, who were always there when we needed them.

— Leonard Lueras and R. Ian Lloyd
July 1987, Singapore